KU-309-307

OXFORD MEDICAL PUBLICATIONS

Ageing

THE FACTS

Ageing

THE FACTS

NICHOLAS CONI

WILLIAM DAVISON

STEPHEN WEBSTER

Consultant Physicians in Geriatric Medicine
Addenbrooke's Hospital, Cambridge

Associate Lecturers, Faculty of Clinical Medicine,
University of Cambridge

WITHDRAWN

SOCIAL STUDIES LIBRARY,
SOCIAL STUDIES CENTRE GEORGE ST
OXFORD OX1 2RL

OXFORD NEW YORK TORONTO

OXFORD UNIVERSITY PRESS

1984

Oxford University Press, Walton Street, Oxford OX2 6DP
London New York Toronto
Delhi Bombay Calcutta Madras Karachi
Kuala Lumpur Singapore Hong Kong Tokyo
Nairobi Dar es Salaam Cape Town
Melbourne Auckland
and associates in
Beirut Berlin Ibadan Mexico City Nicosia

Oxford is a trade mark of Oxford University Press

© Nicholas Coni, William Davison, and Stephen Webster, 1984

All rights reserved. No part of this publication may be reproduced,
stored in a retrieval system, or transmitted, in any form or by any means,
electronic, mechanical, photocopying, recording, or otherwise, without
the prior permission of Oxford University Press

British Library Cataloguing in Publication Data
Coni, Nicholas
Ageing.
1. Geriatrics
I. Title   II. Davison, William
III. Webster, Stephen
618.97   RC952
ISBN 0-19-261429-0

Library of Congress Cataloging in Publication Data
Coni, Nicholas.
Ageing: the facts.
(Oxford medical publications)
Includes index.
1. Aged—Diseases.   2. Aging.   3. Gerontology.
I. Davison, William.   II. Webster, Stephen.   III. Title.
IV. Series. [DNLM: 1. Aging.   2. Aged.   WT 104 C751a]
RC952.5.C65 1984   618.97   84-786
ISBN 0-19-261429-0

Set by Hope Services, Abingdon,
Printed in Great Britain by
R. Clay & Co. Ltd, Bungay

Foreword

Sir George Godber, DM, FRCP, GCB, former Chief Medical Officer, DHSS

The fact that the populations of developed countries have aged during this century is common knowledge, but a great deal of nonsense is talked and written about the consequences of that process. In Britain the proportion of our population over the age of sixty-five will not increase by much in this century, but there will be a lot more over-seventy-fives and over-eighty-fives within that total. Nationally that need not mean that the numbers of us old people who are decrepit and a burden to those in the working age groups will greatly increase, provided that we use the information about health and social factors in society we already have to prevent it. Indeed we are already a great deal better off in this respect than were our counterparts in age in 1948. By the year 2000 we should know a great deal more, or at least those now fifteen years our juniors should, and they should be as much better off as I believe my generation is than our predecessors were.

The main reasons why so many more of us now survive to old age are more social than medical — the sanitary revolution of the first century of 'public health' in Britain, better nutrition, better housing, better education were more important in this process than better health care. But better health care then becomes all the more important because it is more concerned with the relief and control of long-term changes than the cure of acute episodes of illness. For this we need both numerous specialties and good and readily available family doctors, but paradoxically it is the specialty of geriatric medicine with its expertise in social as well as technical medical components of health care which has brought about such an improvement in the care of the elderly.

The authors of this book are responsible for the medical oversight of the geriatric unit in a U.K. teaching hospital group. They have set out to provide a book which can be understood by the elderly ourselves and can help us to maintain our own health. They do try to show that old age should not be medicalized and to an extent we can ourselves determine how great a handicap our disabilities are to be. This is not

Foreword

a textbook of medicine in old age, still less is it a full account of the services which are no less important — nursing, social welfare, and social security. But the book does have the awareness of those components of care of the elderly that physicians so seldom achieved before Marjorie Warren and the other pioneers of geriatric medicine opened up this field over forty years ago.

The last chapter about the future is the most important in the book. But that promising future will only be achieved if society is so organized that the old are enabled to help themselves and especially their still older fellows. All generations can learn something for their benefit from the pages that follow, but none more than my own.

Preface

What does 'ageing' mean? Growing old, or simply growing older? We have begged the question, and concern ourselves with the final third of life, and in particular with what the French would call the third and fourth ages. This book is addressed to anyone with more than a passing interest in their own ageing, or that of their close relatives or their clients or patients, or society in general.

In the main, therefore, this book is about people over the age of 60. The only real truth about them is contained in the old paradox 'one should always avoid generalizations'. For the only characteristic that they all share is being over 60. They are, on the whole, less than 110 years of age and thus have a wider range than any other age group. They have nothing else in common at all and are, arguably, more diverse in personality than any other group of human beings. They are of all races, creeds, sexes, and political persuasions. Some are employed, some are retired, and some are unemployed. Some are rich, some are poor, some happy, some unhappy, some well, some ill. Most have contributed to society, many still do, and a few have always been passengers. Is there, indeed, anything useful to be said about them at all? Only the reader can answer that question.

The theme of this book is that a mature society is fortunate in having a relatively high proportion of elderly citizens; and that a corollary is that we are fortunate in being able to anticipate living into old age; that older people are not only as varied as everybody else but rather more so, since their range of performance in most measurable physical and mental tasks is wider. The average may be lower than that of younger subjects, but this is due to the higher incidence of disease and to disuse as well as to the ageing process, and both the former factors can be influenced favourably by deliberate choice, thereby offering a real hope of a long life of activity and independence followed by a mercifully swift final illness. The other side of the coin is that the rest of society must maintain high expectations of its older members, and must assume that they will be useful, creative, and involved, and that they will continue to enjoy warm relationships.

Preface

Because of the increasing chances of disease in later life, the illnesses that ageing flesh is heir to occupy a large section of the book. Once again, the message is, in many respects, a hopeful one: that many of these conditions are preventable, and are indeed being prevented, and that many others can be treated satisfactorily. That is not necessarily to say that they can be cured, but that the distress they cause can usually be alleviated and that a state of helpless dependency is by no means the inevitable outcome. Nevertheless, the range is too wide to permit of any detail, and those requiring further information concerning the massive problems of coronary heart disease, stroke and dementia are referred to the excellent monographs on these subjects in the same series. The study of ageing is an eclectic discipline in which the pattern is woven from many strands — from medicine, biology, psychology, sociology, demography, economics, history, philosophy, and politics. In a volume such as this, each must necessarily receive less than justice, but the emphasis has been medical in the broadest possible sense.

Cambridge   N.C.
November 1983   W.D.
                                                                                         S.W.

Acknowledgements

The authors are grateful for permission to reproduce the following illustrations:

Fig. 2: after Exton-Smith, A.N. (1977). Functional consequences of ageing: Clinical manifestations. In *Care of the elderly: meeting the challenge of dependency* (ed. A. N. Exton-Smith and J. Grimley Evans) p. 47. Academic Press, London.

Fig. 4: *OPCS Monitor.* Ref. DH1 82/2 of 14 December 1982. *Cancer mortality in England and Wales 1976–1980* Table 1.

Fig. 5: *OPCS Monitor.* Ref. DH1 82/2 of 14 December 1982. *Cancer death rate at different ages England and Wales 1976–1980* Table 2.

Fig. 11: Murdoch, J.C. (1980). The epidemiology of prescribing in an urban general practice. *J.R. Coll. Gen. Pract.* 30, 593–602.

Fig. 13: OPCS Mortality statistics. *Death by cause, age and sex. All causes of death.* From SD 25 1982, p. 3. [In press.]

And what is Life? An hour-glass on the run
A mist retreating from the morning sun

John Clare (1793–1864)

Contents

1

The world grows grey

About 600 years elapsed between the Black Death and the end of the Second World War, and during this period there was no particular reason to doubt that the future of mankind was assured. The principal preoccupation was which of the warring factions would emerge supreme. But now the world has grown up and lost its innocence, and man has learned that his very survival as a species is threatened. We have become accustomed to living under the shadows cast by the spectres of the nuclear holocaust, the depletion of the earth's resources, and the population explosion. But doom-watching is far from being the purpose of this book, which concentrates on the gleam of light that can be discerned within the last of these shadows. An exciting change is taking place within the overall disastrous increase in the world's population: the growth in the proportion of elderly persons. Despite the threat of Armageddon, it seems to be a good time to be born, because the chances of surviving to a ripe old age are growing better and better. It is this change, and the challenges it poses both to society and to the individual, that we shall be considering.

It has been suggested that between a quarter and a third of all those human beings who have ever lived beyond the age of 60 are alive today. It has also been forecast that during the final quarter of this century, the number of people in the world who are over 65 will have almost doubled. The study of demography* is now sufficiently advanced that the latter estimate, relating as it does to the future, is very much more reliable than the former, which relates to the past. In many countries, adequate statistics have only become available during the postwar era. We have a reasonably accurate assessment of the population of the world at the beginning of the century, but we have to rely on inspired guesswork for the breakdown by age groups. The best estimate is that

* Denotes term defined in glossary.

Ageing: the facts

in the year 1900, between 2.5 and 3 per cent of the world's population was over 60. The total population has since that time increased by a factor of between 2.5 and 3, and now approximately 8.5 per cent are over 60 years of age. The total number of people aged over 60 has therefore grown by about 8.5 times during the present century. Between 1980 and the year 2000, the total population is predicted to rise by 38 per cent, but the proportion of those over 60 will rise to 9.6 per cent, so their total numbers will be 57 per cent greater at the end of the century. Similarly, it can be confidently anticipated that the number of octogenarians in the year 2000 will be almost 70 per cent greater than it was in 1980. The statistics contained in Table 1 illustrate the changes that are taking place in a selection of different countries.

Table 1 *Variations in population structures*

	Total millions	Birth-rate* %	Over 65 millions	%	Over 70 millions	%	Over 80 millions	%
World								
1900	1668		c.50	3				
1980	4432	29	260	5.6	158.3	3.6	35	0.8
2000 projection	6119		400	6.5	252.3	4.1	60	1
2110 (projected ultimate population)	10529							
United Kingdom								
1900	36		1.7	5				
1980	55.9	13	8.2	14.7	5.4	9.7	1.4	2.5
2000 projection	55.2		7.7	14	6	10.9	1.8	3.3
France								
1900	38.5		3.3	8.6				
1980	53.6	15	7.5	14	5.1	9.5	1.4	2.6
2000 projection	56.2		8.1	14.4	5.6	10	1.5	2.7
United States								
1900	98.8		3.1	4.1				
1980	223.2	15	25	11.2	15.6	7	4.4	2
2000 projection	263.8		32	12.2	20.6	7.8	5.8	2.2

The world grows grey

	Total millions	Birth rate* %	Over 65 millions	%	Over 70 millions	%	Over 80 millions	%
India								
1980	684.5	35		3	11.1	1.6	2	0.3
2000 projection	960.6				22.4	2.3	3.6	0.4
USSR								
1982	270	18	27	10				
2000 projection	302							
China								
1982	1000	22	60	6				
2000 projection	1131							
Japan								
1980	116.6	19		9	6.4	5.5	1.5	1.3
2000 projection	129.3				11.9	9.2	3	2.3

Sources: *UN World Population Trends and Prospects*: New York, 1979
UN Demographic Yearbooks
US Bureau of the Census
Provisional Projections of the UN Population Division: New York, 1980
Population Reference Bureau

* Birth-rate = births per 1000 population

The old world

The proportion of older people in the European nations has swollen dramatically during the twentieth century. We have witnessed a transition towards a population in which the numbers of people in each decade is more or less equal until about the age of 70, after which there is a decline (Fig. 1). This trend is now detectable in other continents, but it is more complete and ubiquitous in Europe than elsewhere. In 1900, 4.7 per cent of the population of the United Kingdom was over 65 years of age, but by 1980, this proportion had risen to 14.7 per cent (Table 2). In absolute numbers, this represents an increase from 1.7 million to about 8 million. Information obtained by the 1981 census

3

Ageing: the facts

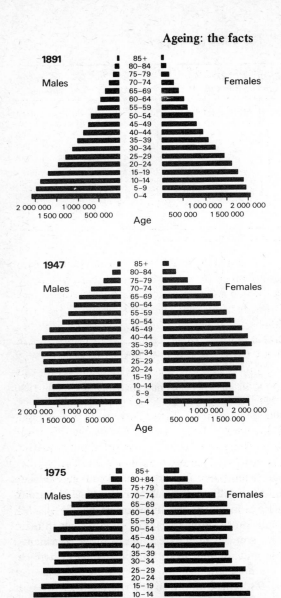

Fig. 1. Population pyramids, England and Wales.

4

The world grows grey

Table 2 *Numbers of persons over 65, United Kingdom – 1901-2011 (thousands)*

Age range	1901	1951	1981	1991	2001	2011
65-69	1300	2069	2762	2706	2365	2670
70-74		1617	2362	2193	2112	2043
75-79	500		1675	1733	1729	1540
80-84			952	1138	1101	1077
85+			569	751	861	920
Total over 65	1800	5452	8320	8521	8168	8250
Total over 75	500	1766	3196	3622	3691	3537
Total population (millions)	38.2		56		58.4	

Source: Government Actuaries Department and OPCS

which has recently become available shows that the number of pensioners (men over 65 and women over 60) rose by 10 per cent in the preceding decade, during which the population rose by less than 1 per cent. The number of women of 60 and over grew by 6½ per cent to 6½ million, and the number of men of 65 and over grew by 17½ per cent to reach a total of 3.2 million. These figures will probably grow a little more during the next ten years, but then fall back to the present levels by the end of the century. But a further shift in age structure will take place within this particular section of the community; the elderly will themselves grow older. During the next 20 years, the number of 'young old' (65-75) will actually shrink a little. There will, on the other hand, be a 28.6 per cent increase in the number of people over 80, from 1.4 million to 1.8 million. There will be an increase of about a quarter of a million in the age group 75-84, so the total increase in the population aged over 75 would, it has been calculated, fill Wembley Stadium or Madison Square Gardens five times over. In the 40-year period 1971-2011, the projected increase in the age group 85 and over is 92 per cent. Two out of three of those over 65, and three out of four of those over 80, are women. By the year 2001, there will be an additional 210 000 people aged 75 or over living alone, of whom 134 000 will be 85 or over.

The birth rate has been falling continuously in the United Kingdom since 1970 with minor fluctuations, and one consequence of smaller families is that the share per child of tending aged parents is increasing. The 33 per cent decline in young people which has been predicted would

5

Ageing: the facts

reduce the number of potential recruits to nursing. Another curious phenomenon is the reversal of the previous predominance of females at all ages, so that between the ages of 18 and 44 males now outnumber females. The gradual disappearance of the spinster may have an impact on those professions traditionally the preserve of the unmarried woman (nurses, teachers, social workers), as well as on the ranks of home carers for the aged and infirm.

France

France achieved this mature population structure before any of the other industrialized nations. In 1900, 8.5 per cent of her population was already over 65, although today the proportion is rather lower than in the United Kingdom at 13.9 per cent because her birth rate is the highest in the European Economic Community. Austria and the Federal Republic of Germany have the highest proportions of over-65s at 15.5 per cent each. In France, the figure will rise to 14.5 per cent at the end of the century, representing an increase from 7.5 to 8.1 million. There are already almost three million persons between 75 and 89 in that country, and over 167 000 over 90. By the year 2000, these figures will have risen to over 3 million and 297 000 respectively, and predictions for 2050 are 4.3 million and 412 650. This is against a background of minimal population growth. During the remainder of the century, France anticipates a much greater increase in the over-60s, but a much lower increase in the over-80s, than does the United Kingdom. There are considerable regional variations in France just as there are in the United Kingdom, the southern half of the country generally having a higher concentration of retired and of very old people. Creuse, in central France, has the most, with 24.7 per cent of its inhabitants being over 65. Similarly, rural areas tend to contain more elderly people (often 20 per cent over 65), partly due to the flight of the young from the land.

The new world

The new world countries remain younger than those of the old world. In the United States 15 per cent of the citizens are aged over 60 and 11 per cent are over 65, and only 13 per cent of Australians are over

The world grows grey

60. Octogenarians comprise 2 per cent of the people of the United States and 1.4 per cent of those of Australia. Comparable statistics for the United Kingdom are: over 60, almost 20 per cent; over 80, 2.5 per cent. By the beginning of the next century, it is predicted that the over-60s will have increased by 18 per cent in the United States, but this is only in line with an almost identical predicted rise in the total population. Even the over-80s are only going to increase by 32 per cent, from 4.4 to 5.8 million. Australia anticipates a 23 per cent increase in its population, but a 39 per cent rise in the number of over-60s, from 1.9 to 2.7 million, and the over-80s will go up from 200 000 to 300 000. If we look further ahead, to the year 2030, the number of Americans over 85 is expected to triple. Within the population of the United States aged over 65, similar dramatic changes are taking place to those we have noted in the United Kingdom. People over 75 accounted for 29 per cent of this group in 1900, 38 per cent in 1975 and an anticipated 44 per cent in 2000. It should also be mentioned that other simultaneous social changes can affect both the statistics and their impact. In 1967, General Motors had a workforce of ten men for each of its pensioners, but in 1979 the ratio was four to one and by 1990 it is likely to be one to one. (In the United Kingdom and elsewhere, automation and other factors produce a similar picture. Imperial Chemical Industries (ICI) now have more pensioners than contributing members in their pension fund, whereas 16 years ago the ratio was about three contributing members to each pensioner.)

The third world

Of the entire world's people 75 per cent inhabit the third world, where overall population trends are gloomiest, with 85 per cent of all births producing 90 per cent of the additional populace expected on the planet between now and the end of the century. Between the years 1970 and 2000, the total population of Latin America is destined to increase by a catastrophic 119 per cent. Those aged 80 and over will go up by 215.5 per cent. Between 1980 and 2000, Egypt will increase her people by 53 per cent, her over-60s by 92 per cent from 5.7 per cent to 7.1 per cent of the total, and her over-80s by 147 per cent. In Nigeria, the overall increase will be 95 per cent and that of the over-60s, 106.5

7

Ageing: the facts

per cent, from 3.1 million, or 4 per cent, to 6.4 million, or 4.3 per cent; the over-80s in that country will almost double, from around 200 000 to around 400 000. A final example is India. Her enormous population will swell by 40 per cent and she will have an extra 31.8 million people over 60 who will then represent 6.8 per cent of the total compared to the present 4.9 per cent. The number of inhabitants aged 70 and over will double from 11.1 to 22.4 million, and those over 80 will multiply from 2 to 3.6 million. (By the year 2000, one in six of all human beings is predicted to be Indian.) The general picture during the closing decades of the century seems to be of an overall increase in the population, mainly in the third world but also affecting the new world, with a disproportionate rise in the number of people of retirement age in the third world, and a worldwide expansion of the numbers of the very old.

Why do populations age?

It is a common misconception that the credit — or the blame — for the rising tide of elderly people can be laid at the door of the medical profession. In point of fact, curative medicine has extremely little impact upon the longevity of a population; the incidence of tuberculosis in the United Kingdom, for example, was rapidly declining long before the advent of effective chemotherapy. Despite modern drugs and surgical techniques, the expectation of life of a 65-year-old Englishman in 1973 was 12.2 years, only 1.3 years more than it was in 1841. His wife, it is true, had fared somewhat better. The main factor influencing the age structure of a population is its fertility, or birth rate, and this has fluctuated considerably over the years. The end of the seventeenth century was a period of low fertility in Great Britain, and early in the eighteenth century slightly over 10 per cent of the population was over 60, a figure which then declined to 6.5 or 7 per cent and remained there until the present century. There was a marked decline in fertility in this country after about 1870, and a further fall during the first third of this century. Fertility rates have dropped again in European countries since 1964-65. The French calculate that each woman needs to produce 2.2 children simply to replace the generations, but with characteristic capriciousness each Frenchwoman is currently only producing 1.96. The birth-rate in that country fell from about 17 per 1000 inhabitants

8

The world grows grey

in 1971 to 14 in 1978. By way of contrast, a number of third world nations have birth-rates over 40 per 1000 (for example, Bangladesh, Pakistan, and Paraguay) which is sufficient to double their numbers in 35 or 40 years. Kenya's birth rate is 53 per 1000, and these countries are all likely to continue to have a demographic structure heavily dominated by the young. China, on the other hand, by deliberate governmental policy has reduced her birth rate to about 17 per 1000 and aims at zero population growth by 2000 and negative growth by 2050.

Decrease in child and infant mortality

The second factor which leads to a growth in the numbers of elderly people in a population is an unmitigated blessing: it is the enormous reduction in infant and childhood mortality during the past 75 years or so. This is mainly due to the virtual elimination of the infectious diseases as a cause of death — an advance which owes more to improved standards of housing, nutrition and sanitation than to immunization, and more to immunization than to curative medicine. At the end of the eighteenth century, 50 out of 100 children died before their tenth birthdays and only six lived to be 60. Even during the First World War, the infant mortality rate in this country exceeded the number of soldiers killed in the trenches. In the affluent countries, this situation has completely changed, so that having survived birth, you almost certainly live out your allotted span unless you fall victim to a road or other accident. Illness and death are increasingly the prerogatives of the elderly, and are things that happen to you after the age of 60 or 65. However, this happy state of affairs is far from universal, and throughout the world, millions of people are exposed to malaria, bilharzia and malnutrition, for example. Ten years ago it was true that in Africa, Asia, and Latin America half of all deaths occurred in children under five. In Europe and the United States, there is little indication that the human lifespan* is increasing; it is just that we are, the vast majority of us, completing it (Table 3).

Implications of an ageing society

Elderly people are much more likely to become ill than young ones, and they are also liable to domestic and other accidents. They are

Ageing: the facts

Table 3 *Life table (further number of years of expected life), England and Wales 1977-79. (Figures in brackets refer to year 1901 for comparison)*

Age	Males	Females
Birth	70.3 (48.1)	76.3 (51.8)
5	66.5	72.3
10	61.6	67.4
15	56.6	62.5
20	51.9	57.6
25	47.1	52.7
30	42.3 (34.5)	47.8 (37.1)
35	37.5	42.9
40	32.8	38.2
45	28.1	33.5
50	23.7	28.9
55	19.7	24.6
60	15.9 (13.4)	20.5 (15.6)
65	12.6	16.6
70	9.8 (8.4)	13.0 (9.2)
75	7.4	9.8
80	5.6	7.2
85	4.2	5.1

Source: Government Actuaries Department and Office of Population Censuses and Surveys (OPCS)

often impoverished, poorly housed, and isolated. For these reasons, they are major consumers of health and social services, even though the evidence is that they are underdemanding. Not surprisingly, it is the very old, rather than the younger, fitter retired who have the greatest needs. The oldest 11 per cent of the community in the United States occupy almost a third of all acute hospital beds and account for almost 30 per cent of the total annual expenditure on health care. At any given time, 5 per cent of them are in nursing homes. In the United Kingdom, patients over 65 occupy approximately half of the acute general medical hospital beds, and almost 40 per cent of orthopaedic ones. They occupy almost half of all psychiatric beds, although the number is woefully short for their needs. In 1978, patients aged 75 and over occupied 39 per cent of non-maternity beds. It can be admitted that even in the UK, we are far from adequately prepared to meet the challenge of a major growth in the number of very old people.

The world grows grey

Indeed, we do not seem to be coping very well at the moment, although for one reason or another we have a low rate of institutionalization with 95.5 per cent of people over 65 living in private households (1.8 per cent are in hospitals or nursing homes, 1.7 per cent in old peoples' homes, and 1 per cent in psychiatric hospitals). It does not appear probable that very much in the way of additional resources are likely to become available unless there is a dramatic upturn in productivity and exports. The elderly are likely to be seen as competing with the young, particularly the unemployed, for both state benefits and employment. If this applies to this country which remains by world standards affluent, the picture in the third world gives little cause for optimism. It is true, on the other hand, that in the non-industrialized nations, up to 90 per cent of the workforce are selfemployed in agriculture and cottage industries, and can then continue to work as long as they need or are able to. In industrialized societies, there are political pressures towards lowering the statutory retirement age to 60. There seems to be a reasonable degree of certainty concerning the disproportionate increase in the numbers of very old people in the world during the next 25 or 50 years. Whether or not this will inevitably lead to a commensurate increase in the burden of chronic mental and physical disability and in the level of dependency, is a question that we shall attempt to answer in the rest of this book.

Conclusions

The world has grown rapidly this century, and the numbers of older people even more rapidly. The rate at which the population is expanding is, admittedly, slowing down, but it remains unacceptable. The proportion of older people will continue to rise.

The developed countries are, broadly speaking, characterized by low birth rates and zero population growth. During this century they have experienced a large rise in the absolute numbers and the relative proportions of their elderly citizens, but little further increase is predicted. What is anticipated, however, is a significant rise in the numbers of very aged people during the next 20 years or so. An exception to the general pattern is the United States whose overall population is expected to continue to grow. Her proportion of elderly and old persons will slowly rise, but will not catch up with those in the old world within the forsee-able future.

The teeming masses of the underdeveloped world will continue to proliferate catastrophically through the recalcitrant maintenance of high birth-rates. Declining infant and childhood mortality rates will ensure a modest rise in the proportion of people over 65 and thus a very significant increase in their numbers. Should birth-rates in these countries fall, the proportions of aged people would rise more rapidly. In these countries the older citizens will be competing for resources which will be very stretched. Here it is China who provides the exception, with her determination actually to reduce her population.

2

The elderly as an asset

Introduction

Never before has a society had such an enormous leisured class. Not only is this class bigger than ever before, it is also more skilled, more literate, more articulate and better informed than previous generations. The majority of the members of this new area of population growth are retired people, the products of full, active and useful lives, a repository of years of experience and practice in achieving, changing, surviving and coping with life.

Surely this development of the twentieth century can only be considered an asset. Yet we concentrate on the problems of our ageing society. We bemoan the stresses and strains placed on our social and health services by the victims of increased frailty. We dwell persistently on the negative aspects of ageing. In our panic and fear related to ageing we may overlook the positive contributions that can be made in the third age of life.

It is true that in a rapidly changing environment, some of the skills of the elderly rapidly become devalued. Practical, mechanical skills can easily be made redundant by technological advances. Although machines and methods can change quickly, more time is required for human adaptation. Skills learnt from many years of 'man-watching' do not date or become irrelevant. Helping, encouraging coaxing and persuading people, are all activities in which the elderly can excel. Knowledge of the past is a great asset in the processes — for it has been said that there is no future, just the past repeating itself over and over again.

It is essential that our interpretation and understanding of the past is as true and accurate as possible — especially our recent past. Only on such a foundation can we begin to predict the future with any degree of success. The clinical picture of dementia provides us with a useful medical model, as the elderly in this state can remember the distant past but not recent events and consequently fail to predict the next happening — for example, if you cannot remember that today is Saturday, you will be unaware that the shops are closed on Sunday, so you will therefore be at risk of running out of bread or some other important commodity. The guardians of our near past are today's elderly, who must be involved with the young in planning for the future; such a partnership is the best recipe for success. But great skill is required (and is available in the elderly members) to ensure that the young are not antagonized and alienated.

Role of the elderly in public life

In public and political life we find the most impressive examples of elderly people being successful in the management of their fellows. Opinions as to whether this is a creditable achievement (or otherwise) depends on one's own philosophy. For example, President Reagan was born in 1911 and after a variety of careers has become the leader of the most powerful democratic block in the world's history. His counterparts in Russia have nearly all been of similiar seniority.

Winston Churchill (1874-1965) after a long period in politics (which included several changes in allegiance) became wartime Prime Minister at the time in life when most people now face compulsory retirement. His most active and influential years were between his 65th and 80th birthdays. He died (aged 90) ten years after his resignation from the post of Prime Minister.

Her Majesty, Queen Elizabeth, the Queen Mother, is now in her ninth decade, yet she remains active and involved in contemporary life. Her example provides many people with inspiration and admiration and clearly illustrates the special contribution that the elderly can make to enrich the life of society in general.

Lord Soper is now in his 81st year but continues to lead an active public life. He still speaks regularly at Hyde Park Corner and Tower Hill, and just after his 80th birthday took part in the patriotism debate in the Oxford Union to mark the famous 1933 debate on King and Country. Lord Soper was supporting the argument for unilateral disarmament, a movement he has supported since its start in the 1950s.

Lord Bertrand Russell (1872-1970) was another aged person who, in

14

the minds of many people, is best associated with the peace movement. However, his skills were much wider, ranging from mathematician to writer and philosopher. He lived to be 98, and even in his final year he remained strongly convinced by the unilateralist argument and actively supported the movement.

Lord Denning retired as Master of the Rolls in 1982 when he was aged 83. He was famous (or infamous) for his decisions. Although retired he remains in the limelight and his views are likely to be as publicly expressed in the future as they have in the past.

Clearly all these examples have been or are exceptional people, their views and objectives varying enormously. Their common denominator is that they have all acquired skills in influencing, persuading and managing other people. Their success is partly due to opportunities to polish and perfect this ability through long and active lives. They have also been fortunate enough to remain fit and active even in very old age, and have thus been able to continue to make valuable contributions to our society.

Role of the elderly in the arts

Old age is the final phase of growth and development. The longer the subject's life, the greater will have been the opportunities to achieve the fullest possible progress. To live into old age therefore gives the greatest chance of fulfilment of potential. Ageing usually implies a deterioration but we should not assume that this is universal to all human activities and talents.

Some talents are transient and fail to deliver the final promised fruits. Usually such failure reflects a passing fashion which proves to be flitting, although a retrospective view may negate such opinions. However, many artists, writers and performers practise and develop their skills throughout a long and productive life. The progression of techniques and ideas then provide inspiration and guidance to others.

What works would Van Gogh have produced had he lived beyond his 37 years, or Keats if he had not died at 26? Suppose Jane Austen had lived longer than 42 years, or Mozart survived beyond his 35 years? It is an interesting academic exercise to consider these possibilities. Fortunately many examples of productive longevity are available and we are

15

able to benefit from work produced at the end of successful careers. Examples are most easily found among the arts, but lifelong progression and development can also be observed in other fields.

Picasso (1881–1973) led such a long and productive life that it provides us with one of the best examples of progression in work and technique. As an adolescent he painted in the style of the old masters. At the beginning of the twentieth century he produced his blue period, then moved on to the pink period. He experimented with cubism and moved into surrealism and expressionism as violence swept across Europe. After the Second World War, more gentle themes and methods returned, his work thus illustrating not only his own development but also that of his environment. Even after his death, with the return of democracy and the painting of *Guernica* (1937) to Spain, he continues to make his mark.

The cinema has been very much a product of this century, some of its early pioneers being able to grow with its development. Charlie Chaplin is a universally known example. Having started in English music hall, he was able to adapt to silent film comedy, introducing social comment and characterization within his slapstick films made during the years of the First World War. Although somewhat reluctant to make the transition to sound films, he successfully moved on in the 1930s, continuing to make films until the 1960s. He was deeply involved in the commercial aspects of filmmaking as well as taking starring roles.

An advantage of advanced old age is a healthy disrespect for previous constraints. Arthur Rubinstein lived to 95 and played in concerts through his 80s. At the end of his career his increased freedom, where he no longer felt restricted by the opinions of critics and others and had reached a position of financial security, led to new adventures in music.

The 'third age'

The third age is a time of opportunity, a phase of life which necessitates review and provides the chance for making changes. Time can be reallocated and priorities adjusted. The special skills and talents of the elderly already described in this chapter are valuable assets which can then be used to the advantage of the rest of society.

Voluntary services tend to rely on the young and retired for their

The elderly as an asset

work forces. The young provide assistance — usually in the form of muscle and enthusiasm — for example, to help decorate the homes of the disadvantaged, to tidy and tend the gardens of the frail and help to insulate the homes of the vulnerable. Such 'youth in action' groups provide valuable services. However, groups like the Womens Royal Voluntary Service (WRVS) deliver a more caring kind of service — providing trolleys in hospitals, meals on wheels and canteen facilities in institutions. Much of the counselling in the Citizens' Advice Bureaux and other information and support organizations is provided by elderly and retired people, their experience of life and expertise in managing people making them ideally suited to such work. A great deal of time is needed for these labour-intensive activities, and it is the elderly who have the time and patience available.

The elderly have much to teach the other age groups. Commonly, the greater the age difference between pupil and teacher, the greater the satisfaction to both participants. The great natural affinity that often occurs between children and their grandparents is evidence of this mutual appreciation. Socrates was 70 years old when he was accused of corrupting the young with his teachings. It was perhaps his success and popularity as well as the content which particularly threatened the security of his political leaders. If the young had not listened all would have been well.

As the value and interest in oral history is increasingly appreciated, there should be more and more opportunities for the elderly to share their earlier experiences. Thus the young can be taught a fuller and richer understanding of our society's past. Contemporary and live commentaries to historic events recorded on film greatly enhance the experience of recipients — especially when they are young and impressionable. The technique can be used nationally (on television), locally in schools and amongst friends, neighbours, and family. Opportunities are therefore open to most elderly people with a desire to recount and describe their previous experiences.

Many politicians continue to teach us about our past when they reminisce after retirement, on television interviews or in their autobiographies. Harold Macmillan — born 1894 — became a favourite political commentator even of his previous political opponents, his accounts and interpretation of twentieth-century history being valued by all.

17

Ageing: the facts

Dame Freya Stark — now aged 90, and still travelling widely — is able from her own experience to teach us of the changes which have occurred in the Middle East during the past 50 years. Pablo Casals (1876-1973) was conducting and teaching the cello until his 80th birthday. Famous dancers such as Ninette de Valois have been able to offer encouragement and opportunity to the young, and although no longer able to practise their art they have been instrumental in setting up schools and performing companies.

Clearly the elderly have much to offer. We must not hesitate to use them. We must not be too proud to learn from their previous experience (including their mistakes). The older a person, the more precious is his or her knowledge as much of it will die with them if not collected and preserved.

3

Loss and deprivation

Old age can be a period of deprivation but planning and prophylaxis can protect individuals from unnecessary suffering. Old age will always be a period of loss — particularly loss through death. Although this is unavoidable its effects can be minimized by preparation. Some losses in old age are more imaginary than real, and these can be prevented by education and changes in attitudes to the ageing process.

Deprivation

The main potential areas of deprivation in late life include housing and nutrition; both are obviously affected by finance and may occur in combination.

Housing

The elderly are more likely than any other section of our population to live in substandard housing, lacking a hot water supply, an indoor toilet, a bathroom or central heating. They are less likely to posses a refrigerator, washing machine, freezer and other modern appliances. This state of affairs is a reflection of lifelong underprivilege, both of people and their accommodation. Many of these people have never achieved satisfactory levels of housing or affluence. As they age their predicament worsens. While robust and active they can continue to cope, but if they acquire disabilities due to failing health their troubles multiply and become insurmountable. In such circumstances of disintegration plus deprivation the need for an alternative environment becomes imperative, but unfortunately coping with the changes and potential improvements may already be beyond them.

The first solution to these problems is political and depends on achieving the aim of decent housing for all citizens. However, problems would still remain, because housing needs vary as life and its responsibilities and commitments change with the passage of time. Once decently housed the options are whether to move as requirements change or to adapt to new needs. Many people look foward to growing old in their lifelong home. With this aim they should attempt to make their accommodation suitable for disabled living. Hopefully such adaptations will not be necessary but it is important that they should be available — just in case. The presence of aids will not handicap normal living. If well designed they will not offend the eye. If they are not installed then the problems of moving house may be added to the crisis caused by any change in functional ability precipitated by unexpected illness.

Living on one level. Loss of mobility will necessitate living on one level. Therefore bathroom, toilet, kitchen, and living accommodation must all be on one floor, with no intervening steps or ledges. This may mean living entirely on the ground or upper floor of a house. A bungalow is not the only option — a flat can be very suitable, although if not situated on the ground floor a lift is essential. If there are sufficient funds and space, then stair lifts can be installed in many homes. If there is access to the outside ramps will be necessary. The access to living accommodation is a frequently neglected aspect in choice of home.

The kitchen. In the kitchen all appliances and facilities should be grouped together with intervening work surfaces all at the same level (Chapter 8), thus abolishing the need to transport heavy and potentially dangerous (hot) items across the room; it will be easy to slide dishes from the area of preparation to cooking and then to serving. Cupboards should be at such a height to avoid stooping and reaching. Similarly, electric points should be plentiful and in convenient positions. The need for labour-saving devices increases with age — not because time is precious but because disabilities may prevent the use of traditional methods. A small, compact kitchen can enable a disabled person to continue independent living.

The toilet. The toilet must be near the living accommodation if walking becomes painful and difficult. A combined toilet and bathroom can provide many advantages. Primarily it should allow more space, which may be essential if a wheelchair becomes a necessity; in such circumstances, a narrow confined toilet may make independence or assistance from a helper totally impossible. Also a larger room would have a greater opportunity for the installation of rails and wall bars. The use of a walk-in shower (without any steps or ledges) should also be considered as hygiene can then be maintained even with severe disabilities. It is easier to survive with dignity in the face of handicap if one has access to one's own toilet and independence in its use. Such facilities have greater value than access to one's own cooking arrangements — the provision of food by others is easier and more acceptable than help with maintaining continence.

Contingency plans. As far as living accommodation is concerned, it is advisable to have a series of contingency plans. If necessary it will then be possible to continue living in one's own accommodation even if disabilities increase. If that happens then one should be able to contract the surroundings to suit one's functional ability. At worst one should have plans to manage in a bed-sitting-room in one's original home, with extra support drafted in from the statutory services, neighbours and relatives.

Moving. The alternative to having a contingency plan for such a siege economy is to move to other accommodation if needs change and disabilities mount. Disadvantages here are the possible delays in finding alternative housing, the upheaval of moving, and resultant disruption of supporting services. Such a move may mean transferring to another district with the resultant loss of friends and contacts.

Within the private sector this generally means moving to more compact and convenient accommodation containing the modifications described above. Purpose-built private housing for the elderly is not very plentiful but some is being provided by housing associations. If a bed-sittingroom type accommodation is needed then charitable associations (such as the Abbeyfield Association) are able to help; the applicant is asked to buy a share of a communal house. The next step in private accommodation would be a nursing home or private residential home. Local authorities are more plentiful in their provision of purpose-built accommodation for the elderly, and warden-controlled schemes enable the tenant to live independently, with his or her own front door. The accommodation should be so designed to contain all the aids needed to enable independent living in the face of physical disability. If and when traditional supporting services are needed, these can be provided for the residents of warden-controlled schemes as well as for those continuing to live elsewhere in the community.

Wardens. The role of the warden currently causes much concern. Initially wardens were simply meant to supervise and to be available in times of emergency, their main function on such occasions being calling for assistance from emergency services. However, as the residents of the schemes have become increasingly older and frailer, the demands made upon the wardens have steadily increased. There is now considerable concern about increasing the training of wardens and providing adequate periods of relief from duty with proper back-up from deputies and other supporting services. If an elderly person wishes to move into warden-controlled accommodation an application to the local authority housing department is necessary.

In some areas new schemes are being devised where peripatetic wardens are employed to keep an eye on elderly people living in their own accommodation, either rented or privately owned, within a small neighbourhood area. It is now possible to install alarm systems in people's homes which alert such wardens in times of distress or difficulty. Personal alarm systems are also available which work through the telephone system and alert the central control office of any mishap or difficulty. The alarm is received at a central point and a previously identified helper living near the subscriber can be alerted and requested to visit. With increasing sophistication of alarm systems and technological familiarity amongst our ageing population, it should be possible for more people to continue to live in their own accommodation in spite of the risks inherent in increasing age and frailty.

Heating

During the winter months many elderly people are exposed to suboptimal living-room temperatures. A survey carried out in a poor inner city area reported that 75 per cent of the elderly live in room temperatures below 18.3 °C, 54 per cent less than 16 °C and a hardy 10 per cent below 12 °C (see Chapter 16).

The situation is presumably better in more affluent areas. Certainly there seems to be an association between poverty, poor housing and hypothermia (i.e. a body temperature below 35 °C, taken with a special low-reading thermometer). However, other factors also play a role. Fresh air has a higher reputation for encouraging health in those elderly people who lived through the demise of tubercular and other infections. Unfortunately the advice for healthy living appropriate in youth is not always applicable in old age. With increasing age it becomes difficult to detect temperature changes, and falling environmental temperature may not be noticed by a frail elderly person, so a thermometer in the room is advisable. The increase in muddle-headedness which is part of the early stages of hypothermia may expose the potential victim to even more risks. Instead of taking simple preventive action, such as wearing more clothing, or turning up the gasfire, an elderly hypothermic person may just wander outside inappropriately dressed and get lost. The physiological mechanisms of cold protection — diversion of heat-bearing blood from the peripheral (such as hands and feet) to the central body core — and heat production by shivering may both become impaired with increasing age.

Protection against cold. The frail elderly are therefore at greater risk and are less able to compensate. If their temperature does fall they are less able to withstand the effects.

In order to protect themselves from these risks, it is important that elderly people dress sensibly — many layers of clothing provide the best body insulation. Environmental insulation is also important, especially the exclusion of drafts. Windows should be double-glazed with glass or polythene film, or even thick curtains. Practical help in terms of money and pairs of hands from local organizations may be required to achieve these improvements. Extra money can also be obtained from the Department of Health and Social Security (DHSS) for both insulation and extra heating. Where there are financial problems it may be best to concentrate on keeping a single bed-sittingroom or suite of rooms comfortably warm. Transferring to cold accommodation for sleeping or toileting can then be avoided. It should also be remembered that a little indoor activity and exercise helps to increase body heat, as do hot foods and drinks.

Diet

There is much concern about the eating habits of the elderly. However, there is good evidence that healthy old people eat as well as the rest of the population. Their total intake tends to be lower but matches their reduced physical activity. Their preferences are also different from those of the younger generation but their diet is generally well balanced. The situation is only likely to change at times of crisis, such as bereavement and illness.

Nevertheless, there is always a constant demand for advice about suitable dietary measures in old age. Because of wide individual variations and preferences, it is only possible to give guidelines.

It becomes increasingly important that excess weight should not be carried as degenerative changes in joints and the heart may mean that these begin to feel the strain. The overweight must therefore try even harder than before to successfully reduce their weight. Avoidance of fat and highly refined carbohydrate (such as sugar) is the best way of achieving weight reduction. Bulk (to avoid feelings of hunger and to provide bowel residue) is best taken by increasing the amount of fibre in the diet — converting to wholemeal bread, flour, pasta, whole-grain rice, and bran-based cereals. Fresh vegetables (including potatoes) and fruit provide both fibre and vitamins.

A balanced diet. Recommended ingredients for a balanced daily diet would include

1. One pint (500 ml) milk, skimmed, if obesity is a problem.
2. One item of fresh fruit daily.
3. One egg daily, or one portion of meat, fish, or cheese.
4. One portion of fresh vegetable.

These items can be used in any way, for example, milk for drinking or cooking. Similarly the egg may be used in cooking or eaten on its own. Additional foods should also be taken and the above list is just a recommended minimum. It is useful to remember that some commonplace foods are fortified with vitamins, for example vitamin C in dehydrated potatoes, and vitamin D in margarine. Frozen foods have the same nutrient values as fresh, but overcooking always destroys the vitamins. Prepared foods tend to deteriorate with storing, except for freezing. Many of the items on the recommended list may be available on the doorstep from the milkman (he may also carry fresh fruit juice, a good source of vitamin C).

Loss and deprivation

It is important that a stock of emergency rations — for example, frozen, dried, and tinned foods — should be hoarded. These may be needed if bad weather conditions, transport failure or illness, make it impossible to get out to the shops.

People who enjoy good health usually enjoy their food. Failure of appetite may well be an indication that something is wrong and a doctor should be consulted.

Loss

It is an unavoidable fact that old age is a period of loss of previously cherished possessions. Many of these losses are very real and cannot and should not be minimized. Those associated with death are the hardest to bear (bereavement is dealt with in Chapter 19). Loss of health, however, occupies a major part of this book. The loss of status and respect is also described in Chapter 8 on retirement. However, the trauma in the last example can be more imaginary than real. Personal qualities remain unchanged by retirement and respect can be gained for new activities and achievements made possible by the freedom and leisure that release from paid employment allows.

There is also likely to be concern about the loss of attractiveness associated with ageing. This too is a false worry, based on comparisons made with the sensual qualities of the young, as compared to old bodies. It should be remembered that functions as well as structure change with age. All bodies age, and we should more readily accept this development. Elderly people should not feel ashamed of their appearance; at the same time they should not neglect or ignore it. Unreasonable concern may prevent some older people from partaking in potentially enjoyable and healthy activities. For example, it is not unseemly for aged bodies to be revealed for swimming or other sporting activities. Some may also be misled into thinking that older people do not have enough energy to join in some physical pursuits. It is very dangerous if people feel that they should 'act their age' and 'behave appropriately'; such prejudices are usually poorly founded and should be avoided. A little of what you fancy is equally true at both ends of life. Attractiveness and vigour are not automatically lost with age, but they may need to be redefined and should not be passively surrendered.

25

Ageing: the facts

The phrase 'you cannot teach an old dog new tricks' also needs to be critically reviewed. There is ample evidence that the elderly *can* master new subjects. When they have the time and enthusiasm their ability to learn can outstrip that of schoolchildren. The increasing number of educational associations catering for the elderly is proof that they are willing and able to learn (see Chapter 7).

Because loss is part of growing older it should not be assumed to apply to all activities. The third age has many advantages (see Chapter 8).

4

Health and social services in the United Kingdom

One of the intentions of the welfare state has been to care for our population from the cradle to the grave. Clearly the architects of our system were aware of our most vulnerable and expensive periods of life. Many of the assumptions made at the beginning of the programme of care have proved falacious — but not the risks of old age. The great consumers of the welfare state are not idle scroungers but the elderly who have been forced into compulsory retirement, whose health has started to decline and who are in increasing need of both financial and practical support. The heaviest demands are made in the final years of life, the 80s and 90s.

How the National Health Service is organized

The National Health Service (NHS) in the United Kingdom is financed by central government, through direct taxation and some item of service payments. The latter take the form of prescription charges and contributions to the cost of some aids and appliances, especially dentures and spectacles. However, the majority of users — the very young, old, and chronically sick — are protected from some of these 'time of use charges'. Although the funding of the NHS has never matched demands, it has been relatively spared in periods of financial restraint. This special treatment has been due to a combination of public goodwill, an articulate and well-organized NHS workforce, and weak central control by the government (compare the position of the social services.)

The Department of Health and Social Security (DHSS) distributes money to 14 regional health authorities, Scotland and Wales. For historical reasons the regions have not received financial allocations which match their population or reflect any of their health needs. Attempts are currently in progress to rectify this fault. However, this is a slow and painful process as money has to be withheld from the richer regions in order to improve the position of the poorer ones. This Robin Hood technique is often referred to as RAWP, as it is based on the recommendations of a Resource Allocation Working Party.

The regional health authorities

Each regional health authority is responsible for providing a balanced service in its own territory. It retains some funds for its own bureaucracy, it pays and controls the numbers of senior hospital doctors, it finances expensive superspecialties. These are the high technology departments of which there will only be one or two of each in each region. Examples are cardiothoracic services, radiotherapy and neurosurgery. The bulk of the money is shared amongst the health districts within the region — normally about nine. At district level the finances have to be apportioned between the community and hospital services. The region delegates to the district health authority the day-to-day running of any regional specialty that is accommodated within its borders.

Hospital services are easily identified. Community services are those based on the primary care team — that is, mainly those run from the general practitioner's surgery, but also including occupational and schools health services. The local family practitioner committee — which consists of both general practitioners and lay members — is responsible for standards of care and monitoring primary care; among their tasks is the investigation of complaints.

Each health district has a community health council, whose role is to act as the public's watchdog. It is a good source of help and advice and is independent of those running and providing the service.

How to use the National Health Service (NHS)

The general practitioner. He is the most important person in the NHS. It is essential that he or she is a person one trusts, whose opinion one respects, and someone who is easily accessible. If this is not the case, a change of general practitioner is needed. This is easily done and is easily achieved without confrontation. All that is needed is to identify a doctor who fulfils one's criteria, and if his or her list is not full to ask at the new surgery for one's medical file to be transferred.

The general practitioner is of paramount importance because he or she is the point of contact for nearly all the services provided by the NHS. The only significant exception is the hospital casualty service, where one may be taken directly in cases of emergency, either by private transport or ambulance summoned by an emergency services telephone call (999). Access to private medical care should also be only through your general practitioner.

Domiciliary services. To look after the elderly person in his or her own home, the general practitioner can call upon a variety of domiciliary services. Nursing help, for example with dressings to injured areas, courses of injections, and bowel management (enemas, etc.) are provided by the *community nursing sister* (previously known as district nurse). The practice *health visitor* may help in providing guidance and teaching, for example, in the management of a condition like diabetes, where urine tests and modification of lifestyle are needed. She may also help in the regular supervision of the frail and vulnerable and thus hope to prevent unnecessary problems and suffering. Domiciliary *dieticians, physiotherapists, speech* and *occupational therapists* can also be called in to help and advise, but unfortunately these latter services are not uniformly available. Other forms of support can be provided by the Social Services department and these are described on pp. 32-5.

If there is a problem in making a diagnosis, then a second opinion may be obtained in one of several ways. A colleague in the practice may be asked for his views. A hospital consultant (a specialist) may be invited to visit the patient at home, together with the general practitioner (domiciliary visit) so that they may see the patient jointly and discuss the problems and solutions. Alternatively an appointment can be made for the patient to attend the outpatient's department at the hospital.

Hospital service. The hospital service is an extension of care in the community. It is only appropriately used when there are insufficient resources available in the community to adequately diagnose, treat and manage illness in the patient's own home. The general practitioner may therefore arrange (if the patient is willing) for admission to hospital after he has consulted with his hospital colleague. Admission may be needed to gain access to diagnostic facilities (for example, special X-rays or complicated tests requiring careful measurements and collections of blood and urine etc.). Specialist treatment — such as operations

— are no longer carried out at home (although this was not always the case). Very ill or very disabled patients may require the higher levels of care only available in hospital.

The general practitioner is not only the link man with the rest of the health service — he or she is also the co-ordinator. He is the only doctor who knows all a patient's medical details, covering the whole of his or her life. It is the general practitioner who can put together the advice received from multiple sources. For example, it is not infrequent for an elderly person to be attending several consultant clinics, all at different hospitals. Such information may not be available at the individual clinics, but it will all be pooled in the patient's file at the general practitioner's surgery. The elderly are particularly vulnerable to illnesses caused by the inter-reactions of drugs (see Chapter 17); such dangers are best avoided if all prescribing is in the hands of one doctor — your general practitioner.

The department of geriatic medicine

The DHSS repeatedly states that care of the elderly is among its highest priorities. Certainly the elderly are the greatest consumers in the health services — both as inpatients (Table 4) and outpatients, and as general practice patients. Each elderly person costs the NHS seven to ten times as much in care as does any other adult. General practitioners receive a high capitation fee for every patient on their list of pensionable age.

Table 4 *Hospital bed occupancy by patients over the age of 75 years — Cambridge Health District; i.e. 6% of total population*

Department	%
General medicine	21.8
Dermatology	31.9
Neurology	12.0
Geriatric medicine	75.0
General surgery	21.9
Trauma and orthopaedics	45.3
Ophthalmology	22.9
Urology	24.9
Gynaecology	5.3

However, it is only departments of geriatric medicine that exclusively provide services to those over the age of 65 years. The staff of these units are motivated to providing the best diagnostic management and caring services to the elderly ill. They have the greatest interest and expertise in helping the elderly; their experience is enormous and increasing continuously.

Geriatric medicine developed out of the chronic sick wards of the local authority poor law institutions, and started with a legacy of neglect and deprivation. It has been a long battle to overcome these disadvantages of birth but results are now evident, although the task has not yet been universally completed. Geriatric medicine is no longer restricted to long-stay care but is also involved with the diagnosis and management of acute illness in the elderly. Good departments provide an oupatient consultation service, day hospital support, acute treatment, investigation and rehabilitation services − all in the district general hospital. The original role of continuing care long-stay is still very much part of the service but is best performed in small hospitals. These are usually closely related to their surrounding community and derive much local support and help which retains their patient's links with their friends and former homes. Ideally many activities should be brought into the hospital to engage the interest of the patients and to keep horizons as wide as possible. Patients should also be taken out on visits into the community − for example, shopping trips, outings and local and family events. These hospitals should be a very special part of a community.

The day hospital. The day hospital functions as a bridge between any part of the geriatric department and the local community. It is staffed with trained nurses, physiotherapists occupational and speech therapists, doctors, dentists, health visitors and social workers. They are therefore expensive places to run but provide an invaluable service to patients who can continue to live at home but also need hospital facilities. All the tasks of the main department of geriatric medicine − diagnosis, treatment, rehabilitation, and continuing care − can be provided on a day hospital basis. The patients may be brought to the unit daily, although twice or three times weekly is more usual. If family or friends cannot provide transport to the day hospital, the patient can be brought in by ambulance or hospital car service.

In the department of geriatric medicine 90 per cent of patients will have been admitted directly from their own homes; the remaining 10 per cent will have been transferred from other hospital departments in order to receive intensive rehabilitation or continuing care. Of the patients in the department, the majority will be discharged back into the community — about 60 to 70 per cent. There is a higher death rate amongst these inpatients — up to 30 per cent. Many will have had multiple admissions over several years (up to 30 years) and their final stay will be to die among familiar helpers and friends. The high death-rate also reflects the increasing trend in this country for death to be a hospital-based activity — 60 per cent of deaths now occur in hospital. Only about 10 per cent of patients admitted move on to require continuing care, because they are left with such severe disabilities that they cannot be managed in their previous homes. However, some severely disabled patients can still be looked after at home, as long as extra support and periods of relief can be provided to maintain the health and strength of their carers, who frequently may also be old — for example an 80-year-old spouse or a 65-year-old 'child'. Such holiday or relief admissions are usually provided in continuing care wards — they may be provided on a regular (for example two weeks in six) or intermittent basis depending on need.

The aims of every department of geriatric medicine are to minimize the effect of illness in old age and to maximize independence and enjoyment of life within the limitations of any unpreventable or irreversible disability.

Social services

Social services provision takes two forms — money and services. The financial assistance is in the form of payments made from central government funds. The services provided are funded from local taxes — the rates — with some central grant aid. A charge is usually made for such services — but the amount paid by the client would depend on his means and the political stance of the social services committee. The director of the social services department and his staff are all responsible to the committee which consists of local councillors.

Local authority departments
The local authority department of social services controls the home

help service, the residential homes for the elderly, the domiciliary occupational therapy services, and social workers, and it also assists or provides a comprehensive mobile meals services. Luncheon clubs and day centres may also be provided or subsidized if organized by a voluntary or charitable body.

Lines of communication are not as well defined in social services as in the health service. People may refer themselves to the department but frequently they are put in touch by a member of the primary care team. When a client requires several supporting services, it is most appropriate if a social worker acts as co-ordinator, for matters concerning financial aids, grants, rebates and allowances. The system is so complicated and fluid that it is virtually impossible for any individual to keep abreast of details. Additional advice can also be obtained from organizations such as citizens advice bureaux, Age Concern and specialist support groups. Much perseverance is often needed if proper help is to be obtained — frail and disabled elderly people will probably need a friend or relative to do the seeking out. Probably because of these difficulties there is a considerable number who fail to benefit from the help available.

The home help service. This probably plays the greatest role in maintaining frail, elderly people in their own homes. Tasks undertaken by this force are very varied, and often more extensive than their formal commitment. Home helpers — usually female but occasionally male — not only clean a client's home, but will also shop and prepare simple meals and snacks. It is important that they are only used to supplement — not supplant — the client's own abilities. Clients with severely limited abilities may also receive assistance in getting up in the morning and retiring in the evening. A seven-day-a-week service can be provided when needed. Fortunately for many elderly people members of this service often perform tasks well beyond their expected duties, and truly become the friend, supporters and surrogate family of their charges.

The meals on wheels service. This grew from the wartime activities of the Womens' Voluntary Service (WVS). As the service expanded, there has been increasing local authority involvement — in some areas it has completely taken over the provision of meals to the disabled. The aim is to provide hot nutritious meals to clients in their own homes, usually

33

about twice a week, but with an increasing tendency to more frequent provision, some clients (6000) now receive meals every day of the week. The basic service now reaches about 3 per cent of the elderly population; it is not free but is heavily subsidized (Table 5).

Table 5 *Developments on community feeding*

Meals on wheels		
1947	300 000 meals/year	WVS
1957	1 000 000 meals/year	
1962	Local authority allowed to finance	
1972	20 000 000 meals/year	
1978–79	25 000 000 meals/year	
Luncheon club meals		
1970	7 500 000 meals/year	
1978–79	15 000 000 meals/year	
	4000 centres and clubs	

Day care. Day care at day centres or luncheon clubs provides diversional activity and social contact with others. It also gives periods of relief to those who support an elderly person. These centres may be run entirely by the local authority, or in conjunction with a voluntary organization; transport for the patient is usually provided, and a small charge for food, attendance and travel is usually made.

Residential homes. If support in the community becomes impossible, the next step is admission to a residential home. Residents are now very frail at the time of admission since improved supporting services can maintain them longer in the community. The increasing numbers of elderly candidates has outstripped the number of residential places, placing considerable strain on this form of care. Entry into a home should be predominantly through a need for supervision because of mental frailty. These institutions are currently understaffed with regard to the disabilities of their charges, and the level of accommodation is very variable, from single rooms to large dormitories. Some are new purpose-built structures, others are converted buildings. The full cost of staying in such a home is now about £100 per week, adjusted according to the client's ability to pay.

Departments of social services are currently seriously underfunded.

Health and social services

Their work force and resources have fallen badly short of their increasing demands. An increasing number of very elderly (especially the mentally frail), changes in family life (for example, married working daughters) and migration to find employment, plus increased expectations from the welfare state have all combined to stretch the present services beyond acceptable levels. An urgent reappraisal of current resources and facilities is needed.

5

The biology of ageing

Ageing is an intrinsic characteristic of all higher forms of life setting a finite limit to the potential lifespan even for those living under the best possible conditions. Primitive life appears to be ageless; for example, bacteria, many one-celled plants such as algae, and the single-celled protozoa (the simplest organisms of the animal kingdom including the amoebae) do not age. These unicellular forms of life all reproduce without sex and they are peculiar in their genetic makeup in that they have only a single set of chromosomes* in the nucleus of each cell. Organisms with just a single set of chromosomes are said to be haploid. All organisms that have natural ageing have two sets of chromosomes; they are said to be diploid and they reproduce sexually. In these diploid organisms only the vital genetic information (genetic code) contained in the nuclei of germ cells (sperm and ova) is potentially immortal, passing from generation to generation.

Each species has its own characteristic lifespan* but there is considerable variation between species. For example, in the absence of premature death from accident or disease the rat can be expected to live just a few years, whereas the dog could live for 10–15 years and the horse perhaps 30–40 years. For *Homo sapiens* the biblical span of three-score years and ten has already been exceeded in western societies and the rectangularization of the survival curves for human populations (see Fig. 14, p. 186) living under good conditions suggests that an average life expectation of around 85–90 years is well within the bounds of possibility.

What is ageing?

By ageing we mean the gradual changes in structure and function which occur with the passage of time, do not result from disease or trauma, and cause increasing probability of death. Death is the endpoint of ageing. Even the fittest of us and those with the healthiest lifestyle

36

The biology of ageing

must in our philosophy accept the fact that we will age and eventually die. There is a remarkable degree of uniformity about the ageing process although certain individuals do seem to age more rapidly than others.

Due to ageing we do not just wear out as we get older: we accelerate towards death. This increasing probability of death with advancing years after the age of puberty was expressed mathematically more than 150 years ago by Benjamin Gompertz of Northampton, England. He showed that the probability of death doubles every eight years in people after the age of 30 or thereabouts. In the developed world we are least liable to die just before puberty. After that the risk of death increases exponentially year by year.

Ageing as an evolutionary adaptation

In biological terms death is a good thing because it provides for evolutionary development and for the maintenance of the vigour and therefore survival of the species. Additionally it helps to limit total population size.

When individuals reproduce there is always the possibility of a change in biological characteristics by the process of genetic* mutation. Some mutants* are more likely to survive and procreate and so are favoured compared with other mutants who are likely to succumb. It is presumed that the specific lifespan* which has evolved for each species confers the optimum balance between the rate of evolutionary adaptation and the advantages of a long life.

In the human the long postmenopausal period of life may have evolved to provide sufficient parental influence in child development for social stability and the intellectual advancement which is the hallmark for our species. This long postreproductive period allowed the longer-lived members of society to act as vital repositories of knowledge long before books, databanks and the like became available. Thus, in earlier societies some older people earned their survival into the postreproductive period by conferring considerable survival advantage on society as a whole and on the young in particular. These roles for the elderly have been markedly eroded in modern society.

Mechanisms of ageing

The biological clock

The fact that each species has its own characteristic lifespan suggests that some sort of biological clock mechanism genetically programmed, underlies the ageing process so as to allow the organism to grow, develop, age and die in an orderly fashion and within a set time. Some

Table 6 *Some possible biological mechanisms of ageing (see text for explanation)*

Biological clock	Accumulation of waste
Accumulation of errors	Cross-linkage of proteins
Hayflick limit	Immune system failure

such mechanism brings about the early death of certain tissues in the developing organism so that natural growth and development occurs. For example, in the developing foetus it is necessary for the tissues between the future fingers and toes to die so as to allow normal formation of hands and feet. In the tadpole the death of the tail and gills is necessary to allow development into a frog. Thus predetermined tissue death is important for the development and survival of individuals.

Accumulation of errors

It has been suggested that ageing is due to an accumulation of errors in the molecular content of the cells of the body. In living cells and tissues there is a continuous turnover of vital ingredients, such as enzymes*, hormones* and neurotransmitters*. At each stage in the biochemical processes there is the possibility of error and if errors accumulate beyond a certain level the cells or tissues will become incompetent and may die. For example, if the brain cells deteriorate chemically, then even if the cells themselves survive ultimately the brain as a whole would cease to function satisfactorily, homeostatic controls (p. 42) would fail throughout the body and death would ensue.

If dysfunctioning cells in any tissue are allowed to survive and proliferate, even if they are not themselves involved in key control systems, death of the whole organism can eventually occur as in many malignant diseases. The rate at which errors accumulate depends partly on the rate of error production but also on the rate of error removal and this applies at both the molecular and the cellular level. In cell division normally the replication of DNA* is a highly accurate and reliable process so that the daughter cells have all the proper constituents, such as chromosomes, RNA* and proteins. However, damage to the genetic material may produce coding errors and result in faulty cell proteins.

The Hayflick limit

For many years it was believed that certain vertebrate cell types, such as fibroblasts*, could be grown in culture in the laboratory indefinitely. The work of Carrel and later Ebling, in the earlier part of this century suggested this. However, in the mid-1960s Hayflick and others observed that some 40–50 doublings was the upper limit for reproduction of cells grown from a single cell line of fibroblast from human foetal tissue. This Hayflick limit, as it has come to be called, is now generally accepted as the ultimate lifespan* of genetically normal human fibroblasts in culture. When cells of this type are cultured from older individuals their potential for reproduction is reduced in proportion to their age. Additionally, when cells are grown from individuals suffering from genetically determined disorders of premature ageing, the potential for reproduction of the cells is markedly diminished. This is seen in its most striking form as progeria (a rare premature ageing disorder) which was first described in 1904. The victims of this disorder fail to thrive in the early years of life and in teenage years show many signs of advanced ageing so that survival into adult life is exceptional. Not only do these people look aged but examination of the tissues after death shows evidence of many of the diseases which commonly occur in aged people, such as atherosclerosis of blood vessels in both heart and brain (see Chapter 15). Also, the protein structure of the body is abnormal. For example, the collagen* tissue shows extensive cross-linkages and stiffening, and there is widespread deposition of lipofuscin* (the 'wear-and-tear pigment') (p. 40).

The accumulation of waste

The accumulation of waste products of metabolism*, either in the cells or between the cells, may well be part of the ageing process. This is

39

particularly so in those cells of the body which do not divide and therefore cannot reproduce themselves. Examples of this type of cell are in the heart muscles and nervous tissue of the brain and spinal cord; these cells are literally as old as the individual. Other cells have a relatively short lifespan* and are continuously replaced by rapidly dividing stem (mother) cells. Examples of these short-lived cells are to be found in the blood, the lining of the stomach and gut and in the outer layers of the skin.

In those cells which are not renewed (heart muscle, kidney, and brain) there is a gradual accumulation of substances recognizable under the microscope by means of special staining techniques. We do not yet know whether all these accumulations are beneficial or deleterious.

Lipofuscin* (the 'wear-and-tear' pigment) has long been known as one such substance which accumulates in cells with ageing and it is found in many tissues. Its origin and effects are not known. Research programmes at the present time are focusing on the significance of lipofuscin and other possible 'waste' substances. It is known that lipofuscin accumulates in the aged brain and can be removed by the use of certain drugs. However, we need to know if removal is beneficial or harmful. The answers to this and other intriguing questions are awaited with interest.

Ageing connective tissue

In addition to the more active cells of the body there is a supporting structure of protein called connective tissue consisting of fibroblasts,* collagen,* and elastic fibres. Ageing of connective tissue causes many of the more obvious manifestations of old age, including thinning and fragility of skin and bone, loss of elasticity of lungs, cartilage, and blood-vessels, and stiffening of muscles and joints. It has been said that it is this change in the physical properties of the supporting structure of muscles which enables veal to be distinguished from beef by the gourmet! Similar age changes occur in inanimate substances, such as rubber, old glue, and plastic. It is thought that the stiffening process in connective tissue proteins is due to chemical cross-linkages of adjacent molecular chains which form fibrous tissue. Drugs are available which are known to inhibit these cross-linkages but their use has to be reserved for special purposes because they are so toxic.

The biology of ageing

Failure of the immune system

If alien substances or cells invade the body, it is for the immune system (IS) to recognize them and to mobilize defences so that they can be destroyed and removed. In this way the immune system protects the body against invasion by bacteria, viruses, and fungi, and also prevents the accumulation in the body of unwanted organic materials. Thus cells and substances which are not acceptable because they are effete, foreign to the host, or malignant can be identified and destroyed. The immune system functions less effectively as we age and some parts of the system, such as the thymus, a ductless gland at the base of the neck, wither comparatively early in life.

With this general weakening of the immune system there is an increased liability both to infection and to malignant disease. Additionally the immune system loses its specificity and on occasion sets about the destruction of the body's own vital organs; this process is referred to as *autoimmune disease*. For example, autoimmune disease can destroy the thyroid gland, the adrenal gland and the lining of the stomach causing respectively thyroid failure (myxoedema), adrenal gland failure (Addison's disease) and gastric atrophy (pernicious anaemia). These diseases coexist in older people more often than can be accounted for by chance and this suggests a common cause. Some autoimmune reactions can be suppressed by drugs, but the drugs themselves are rather toxic and non-specific in their effects.

Because of the generalized waning of immune system efficacy, it has been suggested that healthy immune system tissues could be removed from people in the full bloom of youth to be stored in a tissue bank (as is done with sperm, for example) and so be available for use when required in old age!

Can we prevent ageing? Despite the growing amount of basic biological research in this area, there is no evidence yet to suggest that we will be able to influence the rate of human ageing. However, as is explained elsewhere in this book (p. 72), it is believed that the incidence of disease in older folk can be reduced still further. In this way we can maximize the life potential of most individuals. Good health can be promoted by the adoption of a healthy lifestyle and by the reduction of environmental hazards. However, this requires positive action by both the individual and society (see Chapter 20). Additionally, effective health services are required to allow the speedy identification and effective treatment of disease.

Homeostatic failure

The living organism is an open system which interacts with its environment. From the environment it receives sustenance, but also from the environment it receives danger and threat to its very existence. In order to survive these external threats we take intelligent action individually and in groups. The inner workings of the body, however, are managed automatically by the processes of self-regulation which we call homeostasis* (Table 7).

Table 7 *Some homeostatically controlled variables*

Temperature	Cerebral blood flow
Blood pressure	Number of blood cells
Blood sugar level	
Acid-base balance	Levels of oxygen and carbon dioxide in blood

A critical component of the ageing process is the inability to maintain homeostasis. Normally, homeostasis is achieved by a system of controlling mechanisms activated by negative feedback. For example, a fall in the level of the blood pressure triggers pressure receptors in the main blood vessels, such as the aorta, and this produces signals in the nervous system which cause an increase in heart rate, an increase in strength of contraction of the heart, and a narrowing of both arteries and veins. All these responses serve to restore the arterial blood pressure.

Most homeostatic mechanisms are mediated through the central nervous system and by means of hormones. They regulate innumerable functions of the body, such as those of heart, lung, liver, and kidney. Homeostatic failure is increasingly common in aged people and may be due to age changes *per se* or to concomitant disease and the use of drugs. For example, the ability to maintain adequate blood pressure on moving from sitting or lying to the standing position may be impaired in all three ways singly or in combination. Other failures of homeostasis are dealt with in Chapter 16.

Conclusion

In summary, ageing is a poorly understood complex of biological processes causing reduced capacity for repair, reduced resistance to disease, impaired homeostasis and ending in death. The rate of ageing is to a large extent genetically determined and the variation between individuals is usually small. However, environment, including nutrition, background irradiation, and infections, is also very important in deciding the actual lifespan*.

6

Normal ageing

As people grow older there are obvious changes in their behaviour and physical appearance as well as in their mental and physical capabilities. Many of these changes are inherent in the genetic makeup of the individual but the rate of ageing is also influenced by lifestyle, including nutrition, mental and physical activity as well as by the effects of trauma and disease. General appearance and behaviour gives a good indication of age, but by careful grooming, including the use of cosmetics (and even cosmetic surgery), by the use of attractive clothing and by 'acting young', some people give an impression of being young for their age.

Changes in appearance

Greying of the hair, frontal balding and wrinkling of the skin, together with puffiness under the eyes, are all common manifestations of middle age (Table 8). By the age of 50 the total body hair of half the population

Table 8 *Some general age changes*

General appearance of face, skin, hair, body contour and posture
Failing senses of smell, taste, sight and hearing
Impaired temperature regulation
Reduced functional capacity of organs (brain, heart, lung, kidney)
Unsteadiness on feet
Reduced metabolism
Altered reaction to drugs
Reduced bone and muscle mass

will be grey. In addition to the colour changes there will be obvious recession of the hairline over the temples and either thinning of the hair or actual baldness on the top of the head. The eyes often have a sunken appearance in old age due to loss of fat around the eyeball. This loss of fat and loss of tissue elasticity also accounts for the laxity of the eyelids and a general droopiness of the skin under the eyes (see p. 117).

Normal ageing

Changes in function

Failing vision, increasing deafness and unsteadiness on the feet all occur as we grow older, even in the absence of disease (see also Chapter 9). Taste and smell sensitivity also decline. Taste buds on the tongue are lost progressively from front to back. First to go are those that detect sweet and salty leaving those that detect bitter and sour. Nor surprisingly some old folk complain that everything they eat tastes bitter or sour!

Eyes

Many people in their 40s are unable to focus on objects close to them, as when reading a newspaper. This loss of focusing power is due to reduced elasticity of the lens of the eye called presbyopia. Spectacles may be required for the first time at this age and spectacle wearers may need bifocal lenses. Colour discrimination is less good and there is slowing of adaptation to darkness. There is need for good illumination and bold light and dark contrasts in the environment to allow elderly people to see things clearly.

Ears

At about the same age and sometimes earlier there is a deterioration in hearing affecting high frequency sounds. This is due to loss of elasticity in the inner ear. These changes may be detected early by special tests but only become obvious to the ageing person after many years. With age we selectively fail to hear the higher pitched consonant element of speech (see Chapter 13). It is particularly difficult for the aged person to comprehend the spoken word when there is background noise; conversation in a crowded room, for example, is especially tiresome. Reduced direction-finding ability for sound adds to the problem.

Some of these difficulties may be due to reduced speed of cerebral (brain) processing of auditory information. This difficulty is rapidly exaggerated if the conversation is speeded up, whereas with younger persons increased speed of conversation is better tolerated. Distorted speech due to poor quality amplification is much less readily understood by the elderly. Examples of this can be found in the announcements made at railway stations throughout the world! Another problem with deaf, older people is that when the intensity of the sound is increased, 'to help them hear', it very often has the opposite effect and feels unpleasantly harsh, provoking the paradoxical response 'don't shout, I'm not deaf!'. This 'loudness recruitment' phenomenon may be precipitated by the use of hearing aids.

Noises in the head and failing balance. Changes in the ear may lead to the occurrence of tinnitus, an internal noise generated within the hearing system which can be most distressing to the victim. The inner ear is important for balance and this too tends to deteriorate with age, and together with degenerative changes in the central nervous system, as well as in the muscles, bones, and joints, very often leads to a fall. Not surprisingly, the liability to fall increases progressively with age (see Chapter 11). There is also a decline in position sense which contributes to the problem of maintaining balance.

Posture control. The ability to walk upright rather than in a quadruped fashion is a learned function. The very young and the very old find this difficult. The risk of falling in the adult increases linearly with age and women are twice as liable to fall as men (Fig. 2). In fact, 30 per cent of

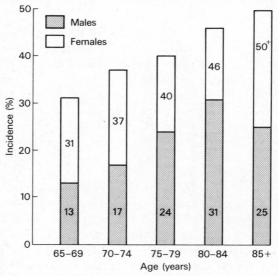

Fig. 2: Liability to recurrent falls (After Exton-Smith, 1977.)

women age 65–69 years report falling regularly and the incidence rises to over 50 per cent in women aged 85. Poor balance, tripping, giddiness, and impaired sight are important causes.

When tripped up the older person is unable to regain his balance whereas the younger person may just stumble rather than fall. Women between the ages of 60 and 70 not uncommonly fracture the wrist, upper arm or collar-bone due to a fall on the oustretched hand. In older women who fall, fractures of the hip are much more common. Falls may have other complications besides fractures (see Chapter 11). Quality of posture control can be demonstrated by measuring the amount of sway of a subject standing upright. These tests show that posture control declines progressively with age, particularly in women.

Changes in metabolism and organ function

Body composition

Body composition also changes with age. There is a gradual shrinkage of the lean body mass*, including the brain, heart, lungs, liver, kidney, and all the muscles and bones. The lean body mass is maximal in the third decade, but gradually decreases thereafter and is usually replaced by fat. This lead to the paradox that people who manage to keep their weight steady are in fact putting on fat as they grow older; but provided that they are not actually gaining weight the fat does no harm and may even be beneficial aesthetically and to health. In women the fat is mainly subcutaneous and obvious to the eye, whereas in men it tends to be laid down inside the torso. Thus, despite continued physical exercise there is a steady decline in both strength and stamina with age. This is evident at work and play by the age of 40 years, is well established by the age of 60 and is much more marked in those who lead a sedentary life. By the age of 80 about half the muscle mass has been lost and replaced by fat.

Metabolic changes

The basal metabolism* (biochemical activity at absolute rest) of the body is highest in infancy, dropping rapidly during childhood and more slowly from puberty to the middle 20s. Thereafter it continues to decline, albeit much more slowly. In sedentary people basal metabolism accounts for most of the energy (calorie) requirement. To avoid obesity in middle age and later it is necessary to maintain regular physical activity and also to reduce calorie intake. It has been suggested that a decrease in calorie intake of 5 per cent each decade from 40-60 years, and by 10 per cent in each decade thereafter is required. Insurance company statistics suggest that obesity increases the risk of illness and premature death. If the body weight is 30-50 per cent above the average for height, sex and age the mortality risk in middle age doubles.

Heart and blood-vessels

The size of the heart shrinks in parallel with the shrinkage of the other main organs, muscles and bones. There is an increase in fat surrounding the heart, a slackening of the rate of blood flow and a slower response to increased workloads. Neural (nerve) control of the heart and blood vessels is diminished but there is increased sensitivity to hormones, for example, adrenalin, insulin and thyroid hormone. Overall homeostasis* is weakened. There is a decrease in cardiac (heart) output, the venous pressure tends to increase, and capillary permeability decreases. There is an increase in the oxygen difference between arteries and veins.

The arterial systolic* (when heart is contracting) blood pressure gradually rises by 20-30 per cent from age 30-70. There is just a modest rise in the diastolic* pressure (during the phase of heart relaxation). There is an increased risk of both excessively high and excessively low blood pressure in response to postural changes, illness and the use of drugs. The blood vessels become increasingly rigid especially those which normally contain much elastic tissue for example the aorta causing an increase in the arterial pulse pressure (difference between systolic and diastolic pressures).

Lungs

The total lung capacity is shrinking throughout adult life. Elastic recoil of the lungs is less and ventilation of the tiny air spaces (alveoli) is reduced and there is less efficient gas exchange to bring oxygen into the blood stream and to take waste carbon dioxide out. These changes limit exercise tolerance, which means that whatever the level of exercise the older person has to breathe harder to maintain the normal blood oxygen level.

Normal ageing

As in other parts of the body reflex neural control is weakened but the initiating receptor sensitivity to changes in blood chemistry is enhanced as a compensatory mechanism; for example, the receptors which check on blood levels of oxygen and carbon dioxide. Elderly people are readily upset by oxygen lack and show adverse effects at above 2100 metres (7000 feet) if not acclimatized.

Kidney (renal) function

The ability of the kidney to filter blood and excrete waste products is reduced due to a gradual loss of nephrons. Each nephron is a tiny anatomical and functional subunit of the kidney and it consists of a filter (renal capsule) and a lengthy tubule which collects the filtrate from the capsule. The tubule is able to alter the composition of the filtrate in various ways to produce a urine in which the waste products of the body's metabolism are suitably concentrated. The tubules join together so that urine flows from the kidney down the ureter and into the urinary bladder.

Reduced kidney function. The kidney size and weight shrink corresponding to the general decrease in the size and weight of all organs of the body. Even in an otherwise healthy kidney the filtration capacity in the 80-year-old is only half that of a young person. The specialist functions of the tubules are also decreased.

Ordinarily the age-related loss of nephrons is of little importance to the individual but disease of the urinary tract, especially infection and obstruction, can rapidly produce renal failure (see Chapter 12). In conditions of stress due to general illness, trauma or dehydration, there may be insufficient renal reserve to cope. Because the aged kidney is less able to conserve water a liberal fluid intake is required especially when ill. Many old people live in a state of chronic dehydration because they drink so little. There are many reasons for this, including reduced awareness of dehydration (faulty thirst mechanism), immobility or anxiety about incontinence. Nevertheless they should drink 1-1½ litres (2-3 pints) of fluid daily. The reduced ability of the kidney to excrete drugs may lead to toxicity if proper care in prescribing is not taken.

Ageing of the nervous system

As explained earlier, ageing occurs in all systems of the body but in terms of self-care and social integration it is the function of the brain and the preservation of intellect which are paramount. Brain weight decreases with age so that at 80 it may be 10 per cent less than at 30 years of age. Some of this is due to loss of supporting tissues rather than loss of active neurones (nerve cells). Nevertheless, progressive neuronal fallout does occur and it is much more marked in certain areas of the brain than in others. Additionally there are characteristic physical and chemical changes affecting particular areas of the brain, a description of which is beyond the scope of this book.

Table 9 *Some physiological age changes (approximate values only)*

	Percentage change from age 30–75 years	
	Increased	*Decreased*
Body composition: lean body mass;		20–40
body fat	40–60	
Functional changes: metabolic rate		
(energy consumed) at rest;		20
capacity for strenuous physical work;		60
kidney function;		40–50
maximum breathing capacity;		50–60
blood pressure (systolic)	20–30	
Brain function: memory, sensory		
appreciation, speed of reaction,		
coordination capacity		Reduced

Malfunction of brain. Malfunction of brain cells rather than simply loss of them could well be the main problem affecting the aged brain. It is known, for example, that there are major defects in the synthesis of important neurotransmitters* throughout the body, but especially in the central nervous system. Impulses do not jump electrically from one neurone to another as was once thought, they are transmitted chemically. Important examples of neurotransmitters are acetylcholine, dopamine and gamma-aminobutyric acid (GABA) (see Chaper 10).

Temperature regulation. Body core temperature is maintained normally at around 37 °C (98 °F) despite changes in the air temperature and the level of physical activity. A deviation of more than just a few degrees is a serious matter and it could be fatal. Elderly people often show a reduced ability to detect environmental temperature change or differences in temperature on different parts of the body. Additionally there is a diminished sweat response when feeling hot and an impaired shivering response when feeling cold. These changes put the elderly person at risk from marked and prolonged shifts in the ambient temperature whether it is a summer heatweave or a cold spell in winter. The ability to control body temperature falls progressively with ageing and may be made much worse by illness.

Sex and reproduction

There is no inevitable cessation of sexual activity with ageing but after the menopause absence of ovulation and menstruation makes the female sterile. There is no comparable lack of spermatogenesis (manufacture of the male sex seeds) and so reproduction for the male is a possibility until very late in life.

Changes in sexual function

In both sexes the libido or sexual drive is attenuated so that there is a gradual reduction in the frequency of sexual intercourse from the peak levels prevalent in youth. However, old age is not necessarily a state of asexuality or sexual negativism and with an active and willing partner elderly people can continue to enjoy their sexual relationships.

Vasocongestive responses of the erectile tissues of the external genitalia in both sexes are less intense and the speed of arousal is slower, more noticeably so in men. In the male the volume of ejaculate is reduced and the recovery time after orgasm is prolonged so that the passage of some hours, and possibly even days, is necessary before he can sustain a further satisfactory erection. In the female, atrophy with lack of elasticity and lubrication of the genitalia can result from lack of oestrogen, and treatment greatly improves matters. Regularity of sexual expression is the key to lasting sexual responsiveness in both males and females.

Impotence. Impotence in elderly people (as in the young) often has a psychological basis or is due to overfatigue or the presence of some organic illness rather than a fault in the 'hydraulics' of the sexual parts. Mental depression can create a loss of libido and anxiety is another important factor even in long-established marriages. A fear of sexual failure, especially after a one-off inability to achieve erection, ejaculation or orgasm may be perpetuated by unkind remarks or avoidance behaviour in the partner. Common reasons for loss of sexual responsiveness are: a monotonous sexual relationship, preoccupation with career or monetary affairs, mental or physical fatigue, overindulgence in food, drink, or drugs, physical and mental infirmity and the fear of failure mentioned above. Good health, sufficient exercise, plenty of sleep and an attractive partner, whatever the age, are the most effective aphrodisiacs.

Drugs for eternal youth

The use of medicines to preserve vitality and promote longevity has a very long history. Ginseng, for example, has been in use in the East for around 2000 years. There are no drugs which have been proven to delay or reverse the effects of ageing, yet worldwide interest in anti-ageing drugs is such that some mention of these drugs must be made here.

Ginseng

Ginseng is called in Chinese 'jen-shen' or 'man-root' because the root of the plant resembles the shape of the human body. Belief in the medicinal, even magical, properties of ginseng is such that world demand is in excess of supply. Ginseng is reported to have antifatigue properties and thus helps to combat stress. Its actions are similar to naturally occurring hormones, such as those produced by the adrenal gland. Ginseng is said to increase resistance to stress and disease and so increase lifespan. However, there is no real evidence for this, although there is evidence of increased arousal and an improved response to stress in mice. A ginseng abuse syndrome has been described consisting of nervousness, sleeplessness, high blood pressure, and irritability.

Gerovital (GH3 or KH3)

This drug is basically procaine hydrochloride which is a commonly used local anaesthetic. Since 1956 Professor Anna Aslan in Bucharest has claimed it to be valuable in the treatment of many diseases and it

has enjoyed great popularity world wide as an anti-ageing drug. However, there is still no scientifically reliable evidence that it has value in
the treatment of the diseases of old age, or that it delays ageing. Carefully controlled trials have shown no ameliorative effect on either
psychological or physiological functioning in elderly people, nor were
there any antidepressant effects. KH3 is another procaine anti-ageing
drug with widespread claims for improvement in many of the faculties
which are commonly impaired by senescence*, such as memory, mental
concentration, sight, hearing, motor coordination and general emotional
state. Here again there is no satisfactory evidence to support these claims.

Vitamin E

Vitamin E has been claimed by its proponents to have magical properties.
Probably no other vitamin has been the subject of more clinical con-
troversy than this one. The list of ailments claimed to be relieved by
vitamin E is a long one, and in addition it is said to promote physical
endurance, enhance sexual potency, prevent heart attacks, and slow
the ageing process!

The myth of vitamin E stems from evidence in artifically induced
deficiency in animals which caused a failure of reproduction. However,
no diseases due to lack of vitamin E have been identified in man, because
the vitamin is present in abundance in the average western diet, especially in many vegetables, vegetable oils and wholegrain cereals. Like the
mystical ginseng, vitamin E is also incorporated into cosmetics and in
this way has been promoted for the healing of skin blemishes and for
giving new life to ageing skin. Again, there is no real evidence from
properly controlled studies to substantiate these claims. Despite the
absence of evidence that these drugs are of value, many doctors and
patients worldwide testify to their miraculous properties.

Hormone replacement therapy (HRT)

During or sometime after the menopause circulating oestrogen levels
fall, but the effect of this relative oestrogen deficiency varies. Most
women seem to have no trouble but about a quarter of them suffer
mental and circulatory disturbances ('hot flushes') and in the longer
term a loss of feminity with genital atrophy and accelerated porosity of

bone. There is an increasing incidence of vascular disease after the menopause approaching that found in males.

Oestrogen replacement usually relieves the circulatory disturbances and can prevent the atrophy of the genitalia. Lack of female libido can sometimes be helped by small doses of male sex hormones because it is this hormone which provides the sex drive in both male and female. There is increasing evidence that oestrogen can give considerable protection against bone thinning when it is taken for several years after the menopause. This in turn should be effective in reducing the liability to fracture later in life. The amount of oestrogen required to do this is much smaller than the dose of oestrogen in the current 'lower dose' oral contraceptive pills.

There has been anxiety concerning possible adverse long-term effects of HRT and these are similar to those suffered by younger women on oral contraceptives. They include an increased risk of high blood pressure, thrombosis and heart disease, but since they are dose-related there is a good prospect that they will be less likely with the new low-dose regimens. Indeed there is a suggestion that low-dose oestrogen might actually *reduce* the risk of heart disease in older women. Another worry about long-term HRT is the risk of cancer of the breast or (much more likely) of the womb. Intermittent rather than continuous use of oestrogen greatly reduces the risks. Death from fractured neck of the thigh-bone (femur) without HRT must be a much bigger threat than oestrogen-induced cancer of the breast and womb.

7

The psychology of ageing

There is a widely held view that intellectual power inevitably declines with advancing years, and this view is often shared by the elderly themselves. The saying that 'you cannot teach an old dog new tricks' is typical of the facile stereotyping of older people so common in our society. It has even been lent a certain scientific credibility by the theory of 'neuronal fallout'. This holds that brain cells which die cannot be replaced, which is true, and that these neurones are dying off throughout our lives, certainly after the age of 30, at a rate of about 0.8 per cent a year, which seems to be in some doubt. Quite clearly, there is an overall loss of cells, but the rate seems to be very variable, and it certainly does not appear to occur uniformly throughout the brain and indeed often spares to a large extent those parts associated with the higher intellectual ('cognitive') functions. It has been postulated that it is the number of interconnections between the cells, rather than the number of cells, which is important, and even that it may be the comparatively useless cells which die off. It is certainly claimed that the connections can be increased by training rats in a maze, with the result that the weight of the forebrain and the length and width of the cortex* become greater. This appears to be true of rats reared in an intellectually deprived environment, whose brains start off greatly disadvantaged by comparison with their siblings (sisters and brothers) which have been intellectually stimulated from birth, and whose brains show no such response to training.

Intelligence testing

Many and various are the tests which have been designed to test 'mental abilities' or 'intelligence quotient' (IQ). When applied to older people, IQ tests tend to be bedevilled by the fact that they are usually primarily intended to assess children and adolescents. If tests are developed

55

incorporating practical information more appropriate to the lifestyle and culture of older people, it is often found that scores *increase* with age.

A further difficulty is that, in common with tests of physical performance, where there is an apparent decline with age, it is far from clear whether this is due to the inevitable ageing process, or to the increased incidence of various disease processes, or in large measure simply due to allowing the faculties to fall into disuse and thereby to decay. The implication is obvious — the first of these factors is beyond our control, but the last is within our control and the second may be to some extent. It is partly for these reasons that 'cross-sectional' studies have fallen into disrepute. These are surveys of groups of people of different ages who are all assessed at one point in time, when it is often found that average scores in these tests decline with increasing age. The main objection to this technique is that these different studies represent groups of people separated by far more than age; they are separated by whole differences of cultural background in terms of education, experience, expectations, way of life, and habits, and are thus not comparable. 'Longitudinal' studies, that is, following the same individuals and retesting them over long periods of time, overcome these objections but clearly present formidable practical difficulties.

Plasticity

Nevertheless, some studies of this type have been conducted. In one so-called 'cross-sequential' investigation, the same subjects were reassessed seven and 14 years after initial testing, and at the same time new subjects of all ages were introduced into the survey and assessed at the seventh and 14th years. The outcome suggested that, on the whole, there was a significant degree of decline after the age of 67, and this became substantial between the ages of 74 and 81. But differences between individual subjects were as large as differences due to ageing, and there were also tremendous individual differences in the rate of change (Fig. 3).

This characteristic of ageing is known as 'plasticity' and applies to most physical and mental attributes. Similar studies have shown that *all* age groups actually improve their own performance on retesting, and training has been shown to produce an improvement in standard tests of fluid intelligence even in the eighth decade.

56

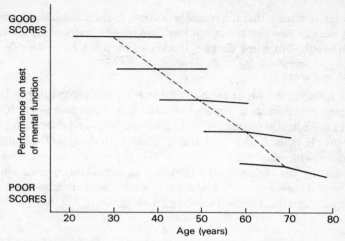

Fig. 3. Changes in mental ability for different age cohorts (groups); because younger cohorts begin at a higher level, cross-sectional comparisons (*dashed line*) give an exaggerated impression of mental deterioration with advancing age.

Some recent research in Cambridge illustrates some of these points. An elderly group was compared to a young group in a whole batch of tests of learning, memory, reaction time, and decision-making, and found to perform less well. But the range was so much larger in the older subjects that in each test many of them did better than the average for the young people (mainly undergraduates), and quite often one of the older ones would actually come top. There was thus a great deal of overlap, and it was generally found that the elderly people who performed badly were in poor health. Perhaps it is worth briefly looking at some specific characteristics.

Speed

Between the ages of 20 and 60, the reaction time seems to fall by an average of 20 per cent in tasks involving, for example, pressing the correct button in response to flashing lights of different colours. This appears to be due to slower decision-making in the brain, and not to changes in the peripheral motor or sensory systems. The older subjects seem to opt for accuracy rather than speed, and take longer than necessary in order to ensure that the response is correct, There is again, a tremendous overlap between the age groups, and speed is particularly affected by ill-health, but some decline appears to be usual from the 50s on.

Problem-solving

Once again, on the whole the older subjects are less successful at solving complex problems. It is arguable whether this is due to a lower IQ, to slower information processing, or to greater rigidity and concreteness of thought. It is said that fluid ability declines, but crystallized ability improves with age. What is clear is that the elderly are more easily 'thrown' by the inclusion of irrelevant and redundant information. It has been demonstrated that older engineering workers have more difficulty interpreting involved working drawings.

Memory

Some differences between the ages have been shown by cross-sectional studies and are therefore open to doubt. There may be a deficit in short-term memory as demonstrated by recall procedures, which involve retrieval as well as the initial reception and storage. This is much less apparent when recognition of a recently displayed pattern only is involved and does not require retrieval. Remote memory remains relatively unimpaired, but, contrary to popular belief, is *not* necessarily better than in the young.

Psychomotor function

This can be assessed by complex tasks akin to the fairground game of steering the miniature racing car down the unrolling track by means of a lever. Differences in performance between the old and the young are much greater initially than they are after practice, and may thus be mainly a disuse phenomenon.

Conclusions

Cross-sectional studies merely illustrate the increasing pace of socio-cultural change which is now beginning to render people obsolescent in their 50s!

Performance testing does show some decline, but this is due to a variety of factors. In the elderly, it is easily adversely affected by fatigue.

It is also affected by cautiousness, so that many do not perform to their full potential due to extraneous factors. For instance, it has been shown that there is little reduction in the ability to hear and understand sentences between the 20s and the 70s so long as the listening conditions are favourable. If the hearing conditions are poor, people experience difficulties in their 30s which become marked in the 50s.

There seems to be some decline in intellectual function which does *not* begin early, does *not* affect all aspects of the intelligence, and is *not* universal and inevitable in all the elderly. From the early 60s to the mid-70s, there is normally a decline in some but *not* all abilities in some but *not* all people. After the age of 80, however, a decline is the rule for most people.

In a well-known study in Queensland, 80 people between 63 and 91 received weekly German lessons. After three months, half of them passed an examination normally attempted by schoolchildren after a three-year course. We have no direct evidence that continued use of the mental faculties ensures the preservation of mental health, but it certainly cannot be bad for the health, and it certainly can enrich our later years.

Personality

Once again, many widely held beliefs are founded on extremely shaky evidence. Once again, the questionnaires in use are often more appropriate for the young students than for those of mature years. It is, therefore, with some reservations that one accepts the theory that advancing years are characterized by increasing *introversion* and that this leads to a form of adjustment to frailty and approaching death by *disengagement* from others and from many of the world's activities. Perhaps it should be looked upon more accurately as a means of adaptation to the rejection and exclusion which society offers to its older members, and to the role which seems to be required of a 'good' old person – undemanding and no trouble to anybody.

On the whole, the capacity for adapting among the elderly is underestimated. What *is* true is that they are less inclined to take risks, and a degree of rigidity is to be found. And another generalization which seems to be reasonably true is that the young regard the present as better than the past, and the future as probably better than the present, whereas, in the 60s they all seem to be about the same, but in the 70s the past seems to be the best, then the present, with the future probably worse than either.

Older professionals, it has been found, are better than their junior colleagues at conserving time and energy and at distinguishing between critical and peripheral tasks. Their needs regarding achievement may have been satisfied, but the need for recognition and a sense of personal worth persists. Men, it is claimed, become more passive, women more assertive in their pursuits.

Requirements for psychological health

These have been summarized as follows:

1. An adequate standard of living
2. Financial and emotional security
3. Health
4. Regular and frequent social interaction
5. The pursuit of personal interests

They may not be very different from those of younger age groups, and they may not seem very ambitious, but unfortunately they are not all readily attainable for large numbers of the very old, frail and bereaved.

8

Retirement – 'the age of opportunity'?

Retirement policies

Germany pioneered state old age pensions in 1889 and New Zealand followed in 1904. In the United Kingdom, at the beginning of this century almost two out of three men over the age of 65 were still at work. By 1971, this proportion had fallen to less than one in five. Retirement was brought within the reach of many ordinary men and women by the Old Age Pensions Act of 1908 which made pensions available for all citizens over 70. During the 1930s the tendency became established to observe the ages of 65 for men and 60 for women as the time to retire by both occupational and state pension schemes. Over the past 100 years there has been a parallel change at the other end of life, so that the age of compulsory education has been progressively raised to 16. The maximum working life of men during the first half of this century has thus been reduced by 15 per cent, and that of women by 24 per cent; 30 per cent of the leisure hours of the adult life of the average man who works from 16 to 64 is spent during the years of retirement.

It has been commented that social policy in Europe during the twentieth century has created dependants out of persons who in the nineteenth century would have been producers. In other words, these apparently desirable changes have certain drawbacks. In particular, a number of sociologists have studied attitudes to retirement and found that the prospects are regarded as bleak. Many people have no plans for social or personal activities and too few have developed leisure activities or been active members of organizations to which they would like to give more time. A sharp drop in income is anticipated, creating a section of society well endowed with free time, but with leisure interests and pursuits more limited than in any other age group. The truth is that for many people of both sexes, work provides satisfaction, a role in life, and social outlets as well as an adequate income.

61

Ageing: the facts

Lowering the retirement age

Unfortunately, the prospect of long-term high unemployment is likely to lead to political pressure to lower further the statutory retirement age, and has indeed already done so in France. Such a measure would not be to the advantage of society as a whole, which needs the wisdom, industry and discipline of the older worker; and the prematurely retired worker, it has been truly said, is a wasted resource rather than an economic passenger. Lowering the pensionable age of men to 60 would also involve a net cost to central government funds of some £2500 million a year at November 1981 prices.

'Flexitime and flexilife'

The hallmark of our approach to retirement needs to be flexibility and imagination. Voluntary early retirement certainly has its attractions for many people. Another approach is gradual retirement through job-sharing, part-time work, and 'flexitime'. It has been suggested that leisure in such large quantities should not be granted us in one great lump, and that we should be thinking in terms of the 'flexilife'. One aim which has been expressed is the 20-hour week, the 20-week year, and the 20-year working life, but it must be re-emphasized that unemployment is bad at any age.

Opportunities in retirement

The catalogue of new interests and activities embraced by those who have retired is limitless, and includes tough sporting and leisure pursuits as well as hobbies, the creative arts, and academic disciplines. Indeed, there are very few activities which are particularly unsuitable or difficult to master to a fair degree of skill and satisfaction after 60 or 70. A fair number of people will, naturally, be restricted by physical disability or financial resources. In most countries there are various clubs for 'third agers' offering a wide range of opportunities as well as busy social programmes. The question is often raised whether third agers prefer to belong to organizations which are all their very own, or whether this smacks of segregation and deters those who prefer to remain in communities encompassing all age groups. The answer is the same as it is in all questions concerning older people: they are all different, and some prefer one thing, some another. However, there is one exciting venture which serves as an example of recent progress in this field.

The University of the Third Age* (U3A)

In a far-sighted attempt to enrich later years, Vellas, in 1973, founded the first University of the Third Age in Toulouse. While it took 11 centuries to create 70 conventional universities in France, within eight years there were 60 U3As in that country. In 1982, the first British U3A was launched in Cambridge and within a few months had attracted over 300 members. It appears certain that others will follow rapidly in many other centres. That in Cambridge bears little resemblance to the French prototypes and is evolving to adapt to local needs and local resources, but has a number of its own guiding principles.

Function of U3As. Although principally aimed at those who have reached retirement age, there would be no strict limits and anyone no longer in full-time employment would be eligible. Indeed, some U3As in France are now changing their title to *'Université inter-âge'* in order to welcome those who have become redundant, perhaps in middle life, or housewives whose children have left home. Similarly, no educational qualifications are required, nor are any awarded. The U3A must be self-supporting financially, it being unrealistic to seek public funding at present. Activities are not confined to academic disciplines, but embrace the creative arts, leisure pursuits, sports and hobbies, and there are thriving social and travel clubs. Research is being undertaken in various fields, including aspects of ageing itself. Every effort will be made to reach interested persons who are housebound or institutionalized.

The proceedings mainly take place during daylight hours, as evenings are not popular with older people. Most important of all, the new venture is a kind of intellectual democracy in which there should be no distinction between the teachers and the taught — there are only members, who are all expected to participate in both, and those who are reluctant to teach can contribute in some other way, such as administration or counselling. During a lifetime, everyone acquires some special wisdom or experience which can be of value to others. Teaching is thus by seminar or discussion group rather than by formal lectures. This is in contrast to the many excellent facilities for adult education offered by local education authorities and by other bodies which generally take the form of an educational package designed by educationists and absorbed (or malabsorbed) by the recipients. These often take place in the evening, they have been shown to be grossly underused by the elderly, and use of the retired as teachers is not characteristic. Similarly, the organization and administration is in the hands of the membership.

Aims of U3As. It must be emphasized that this is in no way a medical venture. Nevertheless, there is considerable evidence that continued physical activity can delay or avoid some of the physical infirmities of the fourth age and even that it may help to maintain mental health. There is perhaps less evidence that continued mental activity can preserve mental function, but it certainly cannot be harmful, and there can be little doubt that social engagement is generally beneficial. It is therefore to be hoped that the U3A will help to extend active life and to compress or avoid the period of dependency, but this ideal can never be fully attained and the U3A will number many fourth agers among its membership. Many members will become infirm with the passage of the years, and when they do so, other members will be able to offer them support. Another ambition is to secure a headquarters, preferably located in a community centre for old people, where third agers will be able to assist in running services for those older and frailer than themselves. It is expected that members will make themselves useful in many other ways, such as helping to man libraries and museums and perhaps National Trust properties.

Membership in 1983 costs £10 six-monthly, and activities include 17 language seminars weekly as well as groups studying literature, archaeology, history, politics, sociology, the arts, science, philosophy, gardens and gardening, dance and movement, and swimming. Some of these groups take place in members' houses, but negotiations have resulted in the use of other premises as well. Once a week almost the entire membership meets for a programme of more formal lectures which have been rich in variety and quality. Active social and travel clubs within the U3A provide varied and enterprising programmes. Warm overtures have been received from French U3As, and exchange visits have been proposed. Any reader wishing to contact their nearest U3A will find the address to which they should send their enquiries in the appendix.

Retirement — 'the age of opportunity?'

Exercise

No one would suggest that after years of sedentary office work and television watching, it is sensible to pick up a squash racket and challenge an undergraduate to a five-game match. What does appear increasingly undeniable is that regular vigorous exertion sustained throughout life well into old age, health permitting, is of great benefit. It is still a good thing to take up exercising long after giving up the habit, but it must be done gradually. Particularly in the United States, we are beginning to witness the emergence of a generation of third agers who are no strangers to physical activity, but this is a fairly recent development. Physiologists are thus faced by the same question that often perplexes psychologists: do older subjects perform less well in the various measurable criteria of fitness because they are older, or because a higher proportion of them have some disease process, or simply because the majority of them have become unaccustomed to exertion and their abilities have thus fallen into disuse? All three factors play a part, but it is the last that is susceptible to deliberate modification. It is the second which is mainly responsible for the greater range, or scatter, when older subjects are tested, and a fit third ager is fitter than a flabby 30-year-old. A 65-year-old man recently ran a marathon in a shorter time than the world record for 1908. The current record may be 2 hours 8 minutes, but a time of 3½ hours, which would be very enviable at any age, would not set a record now unless the runner was over 70, and a competitor of 82 completed the 1983 London marathon in under 5½ hours.

It is worth mentioning some of the findings following programmes of exercise in older people. One investigator subjected 68 men aged 52–88 to six weeks conditioning and found that the work output of the heart increased, the resting systolic and diastolic blood pressures* were lower, the muscle strength increased, and so did the lung capacity from maximum inspiration to maximum expiration (vital capacity) and the maximum volume breathed in and out in a minute. In another 12-week training programme of elderly persons, the oxygen uptake at a heart rate of 130 per minute increased, and the blood pressure was significantly lower at rest and on exertion. In Russia, regular exercise in 22 subjects aged 51–74 resulted in an improvement after three to five years in the electrocardiogram, lung function, balance with the eyes closed, and physical and motor performance tests. After ten years, these tests showed the same average level as at the beginning.

In the United States, weight training has been shown to increase muscle strength and reduce joint stiffness in a group of men aged 63–88. A programme of thrice-weekly movement exercises for 12 weeks dramatically increased the range of movement in six major joints in another group with a mean age of 72. Regular vigorous physical exercise was found in yet another study to lower the systolic pressure considerably, and the diastolic slightly, as well as increasing the maximum oxygen uptake. Even moderate exercise seems to have the long-term effect of elevating the fraction of the plasma lipids* known as high density lipoprotein (HDL) cholesterol, which is thought to protect the coronary and other arteries against the progress of atherosclerosis* (narrowing of the arteries).

It may be argued that many of these changes merely adapt the body better to undertake further exertion, and that their effect on our health is unproven. Recent work from the London School of Hygeine and Tropical Medicine would suggest that health does benefit from activity. It has been found that bus drivers suffer twice as many heart attacks, age for age, as the much more active conductors, and sudden death in early middle age is three times as common in the drivers. Similar statistics resulted from a comparison of sedentary civil servants and their contemporaries employed as postmen. Most striking of all was a study of almost 18 000 middle-aged office workers in the civil service surveyed from 1968–70 onwards. Those who engaged in vigorous sports in their leisure time had an incidence of coronary heart disease during the next 8½ years less than half that of their colleagues. This applied to both fatal and non-fatal manifestations of the disease, but particularly to fatalities, and was most striking in late middle age and early old age. The risk of a fatal heart attack in the group who took vigorous exercise was 40 per cent of that of their less active colleagues. These workers concluded that vigorous exercise was a natural defence of the body, with a protective effect on the ageing heart against ischaemia* (impaired blood supply) and its consequences. They advocate dynamic sustained activity involving most large muscle groups, including:

swimming	jogging
tennis	walking in rough country
keep-fit	walking at over 4 mph
hill-climbing	cycling fast or uphill
running	heavy work lasting over ½ hour in garden

The maintenance of flexibility and balance is as important as cardio-respiratory fitness in older people, and there is a large number of medical disorders claimed to be related to inactivity. They include diabetes*, obesity, osteoporosis (thin, brittle bones), hypertension (high blood pressure), chronic lung disease, joint disease, and disease of the leg arteries. The American College of Sports Medicine advises the maintenance of fitness in healthy adults through 'any activity that uses large muscle groups, that can be maintained continuously and is rhythmical and aerobic in nature' and quotes running, jogging, walking or hiking, swimming, skating, cycling, rowing, cross-country skiing, rope skipping and various endurance game activities. It is admitted that running, jogging, skating and cross-country skiing are associated with a greater risk of injury in the older person — especially if unfit.

Health after 60

There are a few simple guidelines for looking after oneself in later life and delaying the onset of ill-health as long as possible. They are mostly dictated by common sense and do not differ significantly from the sort of lifestyle which it is reasonably prudent to adopt at any age.

Involvement. This implies purposeful activity and concern for others. A reason for being alive enhances physical and mental wellbeing.

A structured day. Following retirement or bereavement (or premature redundancy) there may appear to be no good reason to get up at the usual hour, attend to personal hygiene, dress conventionally, and adhere to regular mealtimes. Yielding to the temptation to relax standards may start an insidious slide into squalor.

The environment. Suitable housing implies convenient location as well as safety and comfort. The ambient temperature should be maintained at least at 18.3 °C (65 °F) and preferably 21.3 °C (70 °F). The common

67

practice of turning off the heating at night and throwing open the bedroom windows is not to be recommended. Poorly lit stairs, ragged carpets, trailing flexes and open fires are all potential hazards and contribute to the 4000 annual fatal accidents in the home which involve persons over 65. Adequate security precautions and refusal to allow strangers into the house are shameful necessities in modern society.

Diet. Perhaps the importance of an adequate fluid intake should be stressed first of all. It is a mistake to restrict total fluid intake in an attempt to avoid the necessity of getting out of bed in the night to pass urine, or to try to reduce the frequency of micturition (passing urine) during the day. Dehydration can indeed predispose to urinary tract infections and thus frequency, as well as constipation and other problems. Some subjects in advanced age appear not to experience the sensation of thirst which protects younger people from becoming dehydrated. The daily intake of liquids should exceed 2 litres (3½ pints).

Other aspects of the diet are mentioned in Chapter 3. It is important not to be significantly overweight, since obesity contributes to many diseases (coronary artery disease, osteoarthritis, diabetes) and limits mobility. A well-balanced diet should provide all essential nutrients and it is now known that most of our energy should be derived from unrefined carbohydrate rather than fat. Such foodstuffs are generally rich in fibre, and help to keep a regular and healthy bowel action as well as offering some protection against a wide range of degenerative and possibly malignant diseases. Unprocessed bran, all-bran, oats, wholemeal bread, and beans and other pulses are all particularly valuable. Fresh fruit and vegatables are also important constituents of the diet.

Finally, communal eating carries the benefits of socializing and is arguably therefore much more valuable than the excellent meals-on-wheels service which delivers meals to the housebound, isolated and frailer members of the elderly community.

Self-discipline. Do not ask the doctor for advice about smoking — there is only one answer he can give. If one has smoked until the age of 80, enjoys it thoroughly, is in excellent health, and has no intention of giving up, still do not ask him: his answer will be the same. As far as alcohol is concerned, the key word is 'moderation'. If taken in excess it can contribute to accidents, and it can seriously potentiate the effects of drugs with sedative actions. Some people become more sensitive to the effects of alcohol as they grow older, especially if a high intake is associated with a poor diet.

Foot care. Mobility is of vital importance, and is very dependent on healthy feet. The toenails in particular often become neglected. If the vision is poor, the spine, hips or knees stiff, or the hands stiff or shaky, then it becomes very difficult to cut the toenails oneself and help must be sought from family or friends. The services of a chiropodist are essential for special problems.

'Flu vaccine

In 1976 (a normal year) in this country, 4829 people over 65 died of the complications of influenza, the commonest being viral pneumonia which is itself complicated by bacterial invasion. New vaccines are prepared each year with the guidance of the World Health Organization. These vaccines afford protection to 60-90 per cent of those immunized and produce exceedingly few adverse effects of any gravity. Immunity develops two to four weeks after vaccination and lasts for six to eight months, so vaccination should be sought in September or October.

Any elderly person with diabetes, a chronic lung, heart or kidney disorder, or living an an institution is advised to seek immunization, and others would do well to seek advice. Egg allergy or a previous severe reaction to the reaction to the injection are reasons against the procedure.

Driving

In the United Kingdom the ordinary driving licence is valid until the age of 70. Thereafter, the licence must be renewed, accompanied by a declaration of health, every three years. There is no legal maximum age for driving. The law requires drivers to notify the Driver and Vehicle Licensing Centre, Swansea, if they develop certain disabilities and expect these disabilities to last more than three months. The relevant, or prescribed, disabilities include Parkinson's disease, any disorder producing episodes of transient disturbance of consciousness or of vision, severe vertigo, severe coronary heart disease, progressive or fluctuating mental abnormality, vision below the required standard (one good eye is enough), profound deafness, and deformity or loss of function of one or more limbs. The best advice is specifically to ask the family doctor annually after the age of 70, particularly if medication is taken regularly. Early age changes which may cause difficulty are presbyopia (difficulty in focusing on near objects) and problems with adaptation to the dark. Diabetes requiring insulin injection must be notified to the DVLC, and driving should not be undertaken within two months of myocardial infarct (heart attack, coronary thrombosis). Older drivers should, in general, avoid:

Peak traffic periods
Unfamiliar routes
Long journeys
Night driving
Distractions (radios and other garrulous companions)

If in any doubt concerning one's competence to drive, it is well worth investing in an hour or two with an instructor in order to obtain his professional opinion.

Sleep

Various studies have shown that complaints of insomnia are more prevalent in older subjects (26 per cent in one report, 45 per cent in another). Difficulty getting off to sleep is one problem, and although the average time taken by a younger adult is ten minutes, at the age of 70 it is 20-25 minutes. Frequent waking is also common, and these periods of wakefulness may be prolonged. At the physiological level, it appears that the total time spent asleep diminishes in old age but not dramatically so; the old spend more time awake in bed, and there is a significant reduction in what is variously called stage four, delta wave, or slow wave sleep (from the appearance of the electroencephalogram), which is the stage of deepest sleep when arousal is most difficult. This may be why sleep often seems less refreshing when we grow older.

When discussing samples of older people, it must always be remembered that such samples will contain a higher proportion of persons suffering from some major or minor disorder. Although disruption of sleep may simply be due to daytime napping, it may therefore also be related to conditions which cause pain or discomfort, or which necessitate getting up to pass urine, as well as constipation, depression, or anxiety. Some simple guidelines for better sleep include rising at a regular hour, being active during the day, a comfortable temperature in the bedroom, avoiding coffee or tea at night or, for that matter, going to bed hungry, and not worrying. This may sound easier said than done, but one of the few rules in medicine with scarcely an exception is that people do not die or even become seriously ill through insomnia. A detective novel or a radio or television show late at night may reduce mental activity and the degree of arousal, and a warm milky drink (or a cold alcoholic one) often has a very helpful effect in those who are not troubled by their bladders. As a last resort, a short course of a mild hypnotic* drug is occasionally justified, but when taken for more than two to four weeks these drugs may lose their effect or accumulate in the body and cause somnolence, confusion, unsteadiness or habituation.

There is some evidence that snoring is commoner in later life, mainly due to various types of nasal obstruction. Smoking is likely to make this tendency worse, and some drugs cause nasal congestion. There is no simple cure, but the problem is worth mentioning as it can contribute to marital disharmony.

'Restless leg syndrome'

A maddening but usually benign condition which can severely disrupt sleep is the 'restless legs syndrome' in which an intolerable creeping sensation affects the lower legs during the evening and particularly in bed at night. There is a compulsion to keep moving the legs and this affords some relief although some sufferers find they have to get out of bed and walk about. The cause, in most cases, remains obscure although it occasionally seems to be associated with defective arteries or nerves in the legs. Sometimes a course of a hypnotic drug at night is helpful. Nocturnal cramps are equally common and invariably quite without the slightest sinister significance, although extremely painful at the time, and the time-honoured remedy of quinine sulphate at night does seem to be frequently effective.

9

Failing health

Middle age: the gateway to old age

During latter middle age (say 45–65 years) there is evidence of decline in both mental and physical powers for all even the biological elite (see Chapter 6). The incidence of illness, both acute and chronic, increases rapidly as homeostasis* weakens and degenerative diseases take their toll. At the same time, there are many potentially stressful life-events, for example, when children leave home, when the female reproductive epoch ends, and when career stresses are maximal; promotion and redundancy can both be very stressful! The outcome of all of this is reflected in the rapidly increasing death rate (Fig. 4).

Life expectancy has improved for people at all ages during the twentieth century but much less for the middle-aged and elderly than for the young. There has been a reduction in death from infectious diseases, such as typhoid and smallpox, just as in the young, leaving the degenerative diseases as the major problem. Degenerative disease of the brain most often destroys self-care capabilities in old age, especially in women. Degenerative disease of the blood vessels, causing coronary heart disease and strokes, are together with cancer the major causes of death. Arthritis, bone disease and muscular rheumatism do not cause death so often but they do cause a vast amount of suffering.

Many diseases in later life start in middle age or earlier. Some are due to the combined effects of heredity, nurture, ageing and environmental hazards largely outside the control of the individual; others appear to be causally related to long-term habits of eating, alcohol consumption, cigarette smoking, exposure to sunlight, sexual activity, drug-taking, and exercise. Moderation of these behaviours offers the promise of better health in middle and old age.

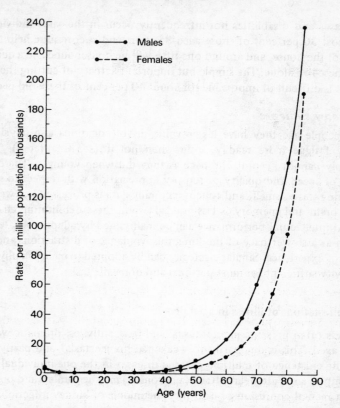

Fig. 4. Death rate at different ages, England and Wales 1976–1980. (OCPS data.)

Disability in old age

Household surveys in England have shown that the most common complaints expressed by elderly people living at home are loneliness and ill-health. Even when they regard themselves as fit the great majority of those aged 75 years and over will have some diability, especially common being emotional problems and failing memory, sight, hearing and mobility. Arthritis and rheumatism with difficulty in walking, or unsteadiness on the feet, affect more than half of this age group. Multiple diseases and disabilities not infrequently occur in the same individual. Almost 30 per cent of those aged 85 years and over require help to go out of the house, and around one-fifth will be housebound and a quarter of these live alone. The simple but important activity of cutting the toenails is difficult or impossible for about 40 per cent of these old people.

Adaptive strategies

As people age they have less psychic drive (conation) and physically they fatigue more readily, even when not ill (see Chapter 6). They simply cannot keep up the pace as they did when younger. There is a loss of speed and quality of sensory appreciation with respect to sight, hearing, taste, smell, and touch; incoming data is processed less well by the brain and memory is less good. Despite these debilitating changes good intellectual performance can be maintained by adaptive strategies, such as a slower pace of thinking, the avoidance of distractions and the use of experience. Similar strategies can be adopted to maintain physical activity sufficient for most personal and domestic tasks.

Manifestations of illness in aged people

Illness often presents in an unusual and frequently less dramatic way in the aged. This is due partly to weakened homeostasis* and partly due to the existence of multiple chronic diseases in the one individual. For example, an acute heart attack (a coronary) may be painless and present with mental confusion or a stroke; pneumonia or kidney infection may simply cause weakness and nothing more specific. However they present, the underlying illnesses are just as serious and often more deadly than in younger folk. Brain function is very easily disturbed in old people so that mental confusion, unsteadiness on the feet, taking to bed and loss of bladder control are all common ways in which illness becomes manifest.

The principal diseases affecting the elderly are the same as those which afflict the middle-aged, especially coronary heart disease (p. 135), diabetes, and cancer. Some show a marked predilection for the aged, such as dementia (p. 83), Parkinson's disease (p. 95), stroke, and (in men) cancer of the prostate (pp. 76, 104).

It is well established that there is gross underreporting of illness by the elderly. Presumably old people and their relatives ascribe each and every

Failing health

decrement in health and mobility to 'just old age'. Even when medical
advice is sought it is so often the relatives, neighbours or some other
person who takes the initiative. Much, but by no means all, of the under-
reported illness could be helped by medical treatment. Even if medicines
are of no avail the old person can often be helped in other ways, for
example by increased domiciliary support, physical exercise or enhanced
social contact.

Cancer

There is a general increase in the incidence of cancer with age and
various theories have been proposed to explain this: (1) changes in
hormonal control; (2) weakening of the immune response to the
presence of abnormal cells in the body; (3) the long exposure to environmental factors likely to produce cancer, such as sunlight on the
skin or cigarette smoke in the lungs (Fig. 5).

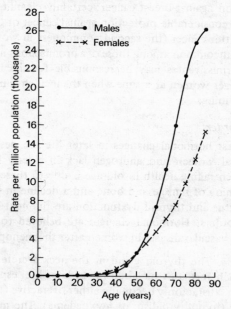

Fig. 5. Cancer death rate at different ages. England and Wales 1976–1980.
(OCPS data.)

Ageing: the facts

Almost all cancers are more common in the older population than in the young. Notable exceptions include Hodgkin's disease* and leukaemia*. Cancer of the prostate gland (at the base of the bladder in the male) is almost exclusively a disease of old people. Other common cancers in this age group affect lung, skin, breast, stomach, and intestines. As with so many diseases the cancer may make its presence felt in a vague, non-specific way and so can be easily missed in the old person, especially one with mutiple illnesses.

Cancer of the lung accounts for some two-fifths of all male cancer deaths and cigarette smoking is responsible for most cases. This cancer continues to increase in incidence in women but not in men, because more women smoke but many men have abandoned the deadly tobacco habit completely. Cancers of the breast and reproductive organs are major killers in middle age, but their incidence is stable or decreasing in older women. It is thought that childbearing and breastfeeding offer some protection against breast cancer; certainly cleanliness and sexual restraint offer considerable protection against cancer of the neck of the womb. This latter cancer (the second commonest in women) is rare in nuns and not uncommon among those of a promiscuous nature. Present-day sexual permissiveness may be responsible for the increasing incidence in younger women at a time when the incidence in older women is actually declining.

Hormonal disorders

The commonest hormonal changes in later life are oestrogen lack in postmenopausal women and androgen lack in elderly men. It is not clear how much failing health in old age is due to these changes apart from a weakening of muscle and bone and a decline in sexual activity. Diabetes mellitus and thyroid dysfunction are the next most common hormonal disorders. Hormonal changes are believed to contribute to the increase in vascular disease in women after the menopause.

Thyroid disease. The thyroid gland in the neck secretes the hormone thyroxine which regulates metabolism. In later life, especially, it may fail to function satisfactorily becoming either overactive (thyrotoxicosis) or underactive (hypothyroidism or myxoedema). The majority of aged people maintain normal thyroid function. It seems likely that both types of dysfunction are part of a spectrum of autoimmune* damage to the gland. Thyroid dysfunction can cause severe illness, even death, yet when properly treated the response is almost invariably good.

Recognition of thyroid disease can be difficult. Thyrotoxicosis (overactivity to the thyroid gland) may masquerade as a nervous disorder or a cancer and can cause heart trouble; myxoedema (thyroid deficiency) causes a general slowing of mental and physical activity and symptoms and signs affecting many parts of the body. Both diseases can be dismissed by patients, relatives, and even by the physician as 'just ageing'.

Diabetes mellitus. Diabetes* is principally a disease of the middle-aged and elderly. It occurs when there is lack of an effective supply of insulin which causes a metabolic disorder characterized by an excess of sugar in the blood and copious sugary urine. The annual incidence of new cases in the United Kingdom and the United States is less than one in 1000 in young people but increases rapidly in middle age to 1–2 per cent in the seventh decade. Over 80 per cent of all diabetics are in the age group beyond 45 years and there is an inherited predisposition.

There is an association between obesity and diabetes in that the majority of middle-aged diabetics are obese, but only a minority of obese people develop diabetes. Possibly in those genetically disposed, overeating and lack of regular physical exercise precipitates the disease. This would account for much of the increase in later life and it might also account for the predominance of females with late-onset diabetes. In the established diabetic, obesity makes the illness worse and weight reduction improves matters. In some forms of diabetes an autoimmune disorder appears to be the cause, and damage to the pancreas by viral infection is another cause.

Diabetes can be a major hazard to the health of the individual, not only because of the abnormal metabolism of sugar but because of the risk of complications including accelerated atherosclerosis* and chronic kidney disease which may lead to renal (kidney) failure. The damage to blood-vessels affects the functions of many parts of the body including eyes, peripheral nerves, and feet. The circulation to the feet can be so poor that gangrene occurs. Good control of the diabetes by diet and drugs greatly reduces the risk of these complications.

Heart and circulation

The circulatory system has complex autoregulatory mechanisms which make appropriate adjustments to heart rate, blood pressure and blood flow during changes of posture, physical exercise, ambient temperature and other variables — the purpose being to direct the right amount of blood to the right place at the right time. With failing health these mechanisms work less well especially with respect to the maintenance of adequate blood flow to the brain. This is partly because of inadequate blood pressure control but also because of inadequate local control of brain–blood flow. Multiple factors are involved including the effects of ageing, disease and drugs.

In western civilization blood pressure levels tend to rise with age and this is partly due to the increased resistance to blood flow through the thickened and stiffened vessels (see p. 48). More serious elevations of blood pressure also occur due to combinations of genetic and environmental factors of to kidney disease. Excessive salt intake appears to increase the risk. In over 80 per cent of cases of high blood pressure even the use of refined diagnostic methods will not establish a cause. As explained on p. 139 lowering the blood pressure by drug treatment can be helpful or harmful depending on the circumstances.

Atherosclerosis. Atherosclerosis* is a major hazard to older people (p. 139). It causes acute and chronic heart disease giving rise to coronary thrombosis and angina pectoris and acute and chronic disease of the brain giving rise to strokes and chronic brain failure (p. 85). Although its cause is not fully understood it often coexists with raised blood pressure and both may run in families. Overeating and smoking increase the risk.

Knowledge of the likely risk factors gives the opportunity to reduce the incidence and there has been a recent decline in deaths from heart attack in a number of western countries, even in Finland where the incidence lately was so high.

Stroke illness. Strokes, as well as heart attacks become increasingly common in middle-age and late life (Fig. 6; also see Chapter 11), the highest incidence of all being in the over-80s. Women before the menopause are relatively protected but the use of oral contraceptives may increase their risk of stroke especially if they are cigarette smokers.

78

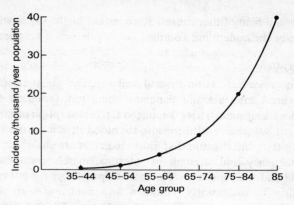

Fig. 6. Stroke incidence at different ages.

As with ischaemic heart disease there are regional differences in the incidence of stroke and even bigger differences between countries. Surprisingly Japan has a very high stroke incidence whereas the incidence of coronary heart disease there is quite low. A major determinant of stroke is chronically raised blood pressure, but in addition all the factors which give rise to atherosclerosis (see Chapter 15) are also relevant.

Muscles, bones, and joints

With ageing comes evidence of degeneration of bones, joints and ligaments affecting all parts of the skeleton. The bones are weaker due to loss of bone mass, the joints become damaged by chronic arthritis which is present to a greater or lesser degree in nearly all old people. The spine is invariably involved in these changes, there is loss of height and a stoop may develop. The bones of the spine (vertebral bodies) also weaken and may collapse causing pain; the intervertebral discs also degenerate, shrink and may collapse and cause pain. Because of these changes backache and pain along nerves which emerge from the spine are common (see Chapter 11).

The muscle mass shrinks with age and there is demonstrable loss of strength, even in the absence of disease (p. 47). Additionally the muscles may become excessively weak on account of disuse, hormonal disorders (such as diabetes and thyroid disease), lack of vitamin D, drug treatment and many other causes. Recognition of the cause will allow correction of the underlying disorder.

Digestive system

There is decreased secretion of acid and digestive juices affecting the stomach, small intestine and pancreas; the latter produces digestive juices as well as insulin. There is reduced active absorption of substances from the gut but passive diffusion into the blood stream is little affected; it is by this latter mechanism that most medicines are absorbed.

The frequency and strength of intestinal muscle contractions are diminished and the time taken for food to pass along the gut is longer. Constipation is increasingly common and contributes to ill-health because piles (haemorrhoids*), ruptures (hernias*), and diverticular disease may develop. The latter condition which affects the large bowel is rare in countries where a high-fibre (residue) diet is usual but very common in western society with its low-fibre diet. The walls of the large bowel (colon) develop outpouchings which may become inflamed or obstruct causing a wide variety of symptoms and signs. Constipation, and its evil sequelae, can be avoided by good lifelong habits of eating, regular exercise, plentiful fluids, and the avoidance of drugs which affect bowel function (see also Chapter 14).

Attitudes to failing health

Any description of failing health in later life is almost bound to have a pessimistic flavour. The possibility of increased dependence on others is a great worry to most elderly people but for some it is welcomed because of the attention and relief from boredom which illness can bring. For the majority, however, there can be no passive surrender to the processes and diseases of ageing. Even the most aged will be actively engaged in grappling with life's problems in as much as they are able; those who support them must encourage independent activity and not overprotect. Drug and other therapies will be much more helpful if plentiful mental and social stimulation are also present. It has been said that nothing promotes the welfare of older folk as effectively as asking something of them and expecting them to be able to do what is asked. This applies equally to those whose health is failing but the demands made must be within the range of the possible; the principle is the same for us all.

What has medicine to offer?

It will be evident from this chapter and from Chapters 8 and 20, as well as from information elsewhere in this book that much can be done to improve health in later life by the early adoption of a prudent lifestyle with respect to mental, social and physical activities. For those already old and ill medicine may have much to offer and one must not too readily ascribe lack of capability merely to old age.

Many of the diseases of old age are curable, or at least treatable, to the extent that there can be considerable symptomatic relief as well as improved function. For example, some of the autoimmune diseases, such as thyrotoxicosis, thyroid failure, and pernicious anaemia are all eminently treatable; other examples are certain inflammatory diseases of blood-vessels, some severe forms of muscular rheumatism and many common infections, and even some common cancers, especially those affecting the skin.

When health falters there is need for a careful appraisal of the whole problem and a carefully balanced approach to treatment. This allows treatment to be given where it is most likely to do good. The doctor has to work within the bounds of what is possible with respect to drugs and other treatments. For example, we have no cure yet for most forms of arthritis, but much can be done with drugs and a regimen of exercises to minimize pain and disability. Unfortunately some of the more effective drugs for damping down the inflammation of the joints can upset the stomach. It may be necessary to accept a compromise.

Failing health in middle and old age may not be as inevitable as was once thought or at any rate need not come on so severely or so early. The lifelong cultivation of a healthy active mind and body offers the best prospect for a healthy old age; but if illness does strike modern medicine has much to offer.

10

Mental disorders

Mental ill-health in later life is very common, causes much suffering, and has an enormous impact on families, friends, neighbours, and the statutory services. It is dominated by failure of the brain and depression.

Brain failure

When someone is a competent, independent member of society but then abruptly becomes confused and disorientated, we speak of acute brain failure. When, over a period of many months, she becomes increasingly vague and forgetful and unable to manage her house or herself, we regard her as having chronic brain failure.

Acute brain failure

An acute confusional state, or delirium, is a dramatic and distressing event in which the patient becomes agitated and restless with fluctuating misinterpretation of events and surroundings. At times there may even be clouding of the consciousness, and at other times there may be intervals of lucidity. There are frequently hallucinations, in which the patient is disturbed by visions of totally non-existent persons or creatures, and delusions, in which everyday sights such as regular visitors are the subject of sinister misidentification. The condition is not truly a mental illness, but a common manifestation of acute physical disease, although it is probably more likely to occur in those who have a mild degree of brain disease and who are thus at risk even if normally well compensated. The main causes of an acute toxic psychosis are as follows:

Drugs: for Parkinson's disease, steroids, narcotics
Infections: pneumonia, urinary tract infections
Cardiac: heart failure, heart attack, change of rate or rhythm

Metabolic: low blood sugar (hypoglycaemia), respiratory failure (see Chapter 15)

Intracranial: stroke, viral meningoencephalitis (serious brain disease)

Treatment. Sedation may be necessary while the underlying disease is diagnosed and treated. Unfortunately, removal to the strange faces and surroundings of a hospital may well make matters considerably worse in the short term.

Chronic brain failure: dementia

Dementia may be defined as a global impairment of every aspect of the intelligence, memory and personality without any alteration of consciousness.

Incidence. The illness afflicts between 5 and 10 per cent of people over the age of 65, but the incidence rises with age so that no less than 20 per cent of persons over 80 are affected. The total of significantly affected sufferers in the United Kingdom is estimated to be about three-quarters of a million.

Characteristics of the disease. The condition is progressive. In the early stages, insight is usually preserved and this may lead to profound depression and anxiety, but then some or all of the following features become apparent:

Loss of power of concentration and attention
Grossly reduced capacity for new learning
Loss of memory, initially recent but later long term
Behaviour may deteriorate and become disinhibited, noisy, antisocial, dirty, aggressive
Confusion, disorientation, poor grasp of circumstances
Restlessness, wandering, self-neglect
Incontinence and immobility
Apathy, inability to converse, difficult to engage attention, plucking at clothing

Although some of the sufferers are depressed, many do not pass through this phase but may remain quite cheerful, while in others, apathy and mental vegetation predominate. From the point of view of the family, the disease may be exceedingly distressing as well as most trying. It is completely destructive of the patient as a person, and to have a demented spouse is to be bereaved without being widowed. The stage of nocturnal restlessness is particularly difficult, and the patient may get dressed at 2 a.m. to go to work or may indulge in mindless, quasipurposeful activities such as rummaging in drawers. Social competence and the capacity for self-care are quickly eroded, and those who live alone become liable to malnutrition, dehydration, hypothermia, bronchopneumonia, falls and other domestic accidents. The course of the disease is very variable, but although fatal it often takes many months or years.

Diagnosis. It will readily be appreciated that diagnosis, in the early stages, may be extremely difficult for the family, for friends, and for the physician. The pitfall to be avoided at all costs is to mistake eccentricity for early dementia. In particular, although most people remain reasonably fastidious in their care of themselves and their surroundings, some do not but allow first their homes and then their clothing and their bodies to become neglected, unkempt and unhygienic in their old age. This may occur despite an entirely lucid and active mind, and is sometimes called the 'senile squalor syndrome', and leads to great anxiety on the part of the relatives and neighbours who may make well-meaning but mistaken representations to the health or social services to the effect that 'something must be done'. Advanced self-neglect, filth and degradation, with hoarding of mountains of rubbish, in isolated, totally unrepentant people of sound mind, is sometimes termed the 'Diogenes syndrome' after the Greek philosopher noted for his contempt of the social niceties.

There are many other pitfalls when trying to assess the mental competence of those much older than oneself. When one day is much like another, it is excusable to be unaware of the day of the week. When one government is much like another, it is excusable to forget names which are currently in the news. Problems with hearing and vision may make communication difficult, and speech disabilities arising from a stroke may make it impossible. Finally, depression can lead to a state of withdrawal and inability to cope with life.

It should also be mentioned that dementia, with disintegration of

84

intellect and personality is, rarely, the result of a physical, potentially remediable, disease. Chronic drug toxicity, certain vitamin deficiencies (notably B_{12}), underactivity of the thyroid, and tumours compressing the brain may all cause this picture, sometimes with very few other features. Ideally, before making a firm diagnosis of irreversible dementia, the doctor should arrange for the brain to be imaged by means of computerized tomographic (CT) scanning, an entirely risk-free technique pioneered by the British company EMI. Regrettably, resources within the NHS do not permit achievement of this counsel of perfection in the majority of cases.

Cause of dementia. Despite what has been said concerning the rising incidence with advancing age, dementia is a disease process and is *not* an inevitable accompaniment of old age. There are two varieties — senile dementia (Alzheimer type) and multi-infarct disease which account for approximately 50 per cent and 30 per cent of cases respectively, the remaining 20 per cent showing a mixed picture.

In Alzheimer-type dementia, examination of the brain after death shows diffuse loss of the cerebral cortex* (the grey matter). These patients pursue a progressively downhill course. The cause remains obscure, although at a chemical level there is no doubt that there is a deficiency of the enzyme* choline acetyl transferase which is required for the production of the neurotransmitter* acetylcholine, and which probably reflects loss of nerve cells in the cortex and in a certain part of the brain stem. This finding offers some hope that the course of the disease might be modified by replacement of the deficient chemical as has proved so spectacularly possible in Parkinson's disease (see Chapter 11). Heredity may play a part and there is a familial tendency although the disease is not directly inherited. It may conceivably be due to a slow virus infection, and there is certainly a single recorded instance of an exceedingly rare related disorder being transmitted from one human subject to another by corneal grafting from an affected donor.

In multi-infarct disease, there are multiple cerebral softenings or infarcts* (areas of tissue death) due to inadequate blood supply. Progress during life is therefore by a series of fairly sudden downhill steps, with perhaps identifiable minor or even major strokes (see Chapter 11). Males are proportionately more frequently affected, in contrast to Alzheimer's disease, and it often occurs at a rather earlier age. Because arterial disease is the underlying cause, it is commoner in those who have suffered from hypertension. Difficulties with walking, swallowing, and controlling the emotions are sometimes encountered in these patients.

Treatment of dementia. Apart from the small minority with a treatable underlying cause, medical measures have very little to offer beyond the occasional use of hypnotics and tranquillizers to control restlessness and aggression. The doctor does have an essential role in establishing the diagnosis and advising and supporting the relatives. Permanent institutional care is ultimately required in advanced cases needing continuous supervision, but provision is scarce. The less severely afflicted should be given every encouragement to stay at home, especially if fortunate enough to have a supportive family. This will require the usual supporting services (home help, meals-on-wheels) for those living alone or with frail spouses. After the early stages, living alone becomes impossible, and families will be able to cope much longer if early help is offered in the form of day care two or three times a week, or short-term relief admission to an institution to enable them to take a much-needed and well-deserved holiday.

Whether the solution is day care, or short-term or prolonged institutional care, there is often a question as to which is the appropriate authority to turn to. This differs according to locality but in general it may be said that when physical dependency dominates the picture, the responsibility will be that of the geriatric service. When the subject is reasonably able-bodied (able to walk) but demented, it will depend on whether behaviour is antisocial or not: severely disturbed patients require the skills of the psychiatric service, but the 'happy wanderer' should be perfectly manageable in the setting of a local authority old people's home. Some local authorities run separate facilities for the 'elderly mentally infirm', but others integrate them into their ordinary homes.

In spite of the theoretically comprehensive services described, it must be added that there is no evidence that either the health or the social services are about to rectify the growing deficiences in provision, and there are at least five significantly demented patients in the community for every one in hospital. A further 100 000 moderately to

86

severely demented aged people are anticipated in this country by the end of the century. For legal aspects of testamentary incapacity see Chapter 19, but it may be mentioned here that there are provisions under the Mental Health Act whereby compulsory admission can be arranged upon application by a relative or social worker for variable periods depending on the particular section of the act invoked and the number of doctors making the order. Such a step is very much a last resort and doctors and social workers and enlightened members of the public are most reluctant to detain people against their wishes unless it is essential for their own or, even less often, other people's safety.

Depression

Depressive illness in older people is also common and causes much suffering and even death. Some surveys have suggested that up to 15 per cent of people over 65 are moderately or severely depressed. Contrary to popular belief, suicide is commonplace in this age group which accounts for 25-30 per cent of cases. Attempts are probably more often successful among older people because many live alone and are found too late, and because resuscitation is more difficult. The outlook is otherwise, however, really very favourable in at least a third of cases with a tendency towards spontaneous improvement or a good response to treatment but a liability to recurrence. In contrast to other European countries, suicide rates have fallen substantially in England, Wales, and Greece since the early 1960s, and this decline is most marked in the elderly. Elsewhere in Europe, their suicide rate is increasing along with that of their younger compatriots.

Principal features. Depression can be a dreadful disease, and the patient may exhibit any combination of the following features:

Sadness, hopelessness, silent misery
Anxiety, obsessiveness
Loss of interests, energy, concentration and memory
Sleep disturbance, early waking
Off food, off drink, general health failing
Ideas of guilt, self-reproach

Preoccupation with real or imaginary physical disorders, hypochondriasis

Retardation (slowing of movement, speech and responsiveness)

Agitation (restlessness, trembling, demanding manner)

Delusions, hallucinations

Suicidal preoccupations

Diminished libido

Cause. This is basically obscure, although there is a strong association with physical disease. At the level of cellular chemistry there appears to be depletion of the neurotransmitters* serotonin, adrenalin, and noradrenalin in the brain.

Diagnosis. Detection presents surprising difficulties, and according to one survey 72 per cent of cases in the community are not recognized by their family doctors. Admission to hospital for this illness is fairly uncommon in older subjects compared to younger ones. This is partly because the sufferer is often too withdrawn to seek advice, and partly because the disease closely mimics many physical conditions. All too often, it is because relatives, friends, and even doctors take the attitude that elderly persons are subject to bereavement, separation from children, loss of status and income and failing health, so that a degree of depression is perfectly normal. Most people, however, overcome grief and sorrow without becoming abnormally depressed.

Treatment. The usual treatment is the prescription of antidepressant drugs which appear to potentiate the action of these neurotransmitters by inhibiting the cells from returning them into storage. They generally require two weeks or more to become effective, and may take longer if the dose needs to be increased because it is prudent to start with a low dose. This is because most of them may occasionally produce adverse effects such as drowsiness, confusion, constipation, difficulty in passing urine, dryness of the mouth, and blurring of vision. Some of these drugs can be given in a single dose at night in order to promote sleep and reduce daytime sedation. Although there is a large number of available preparations, the best are probably *amitriptyline* (e.g. Tryptizol), *mianserin* (e.g. Bolvidon, Norval) (both particularly useful in agitated depression), *imipramine* (e.g. Tofranil) (for the more retarded or withdrawn and apathetic patient), and *dothiepin* (e.g. Prothiaden) (for the mixed picture).

Patients who do not respond are at risk from suicide, malnutrition, dehydration, and the bedridden state, and may suffer from persistent delusions that they are evil and deserve to die. Notwithstanding the adverse publicity which it has received, electroconvulsive therapy (ECT) usually affords rapid and effective relief. This treatment is never embarked upon lightly, and consists of applying an electrical current to the temples which would be strong enough to produce a convulsion if this were not forestalled by the use of muscle-relaxant drugs. The treatment is very safe, any confusion or impairment of memory afterwards usually being shortlived.

Anxiety states

Anxiety is a common feature of depression, dementia, and physical illness, and often affects persons of all ages, young as well as old, who have none of these things. Sometimes it is permissible to wonder whether it would be normal if the old, the frail, the isolated, and the impoverished were *not* anxious, or, for that matter, frankly depressed. Anxiety states occurring in isolation are less common than depressive illness, but may lead to a degree of depression, and may commonly produce physical symptoms such as palpitations, breathlessness, giddiness, and abdominal discomfort. The condition may respond to the doctor's reassurance, or, better still, to the relief of loneliness if this can be achieved. Otherwise, a short course of a minor tranquillizer such as *diazepam* (Valium) may be useful but the dose should be a low one and never exceeded by the patient. A gentle hypnotic may be required at night, and drugs which can be recommended, with reservations (see the section on sleep in Chapter 8), are *chlormethiazole* (Heminevrin) *dichloralphenazone* (Welldorm), and *temazepam* (Euhypnos).

Institutional neurosis

Institutional neurosis is the term given to the state of apathy and passive acceptance found in those consigned by society to long-term care. Now that the days of prolonged residence of young people in mental hospitals are over, the condition has become very much the preserve of the very old, and even today those who visit extended care geriatric wards may encounter the sight of the inmates sitting round the walls of the day room in silent inactivity. However great the efforts made by the staff and by voluntary workers, this is still a powerful argument for delaying, or, better still, avoiding custodial care.

Other mental disorders such as schizophrenia and alcoholism are to be found in older people just as in other age groups, but will not be discussed here because they do not relate to the theme of ageing as such.

11

Mobility and immobility

If mobility is lost, an independent life is impossible, unless a mechanical substitute for walking and transferring (i.e. moving from chair to bed, etc.) can be devised. Like most of the good things in life, our ability to walk without effort or thought is only appreciated when threatened or lost.

Walking may be compromised because of weakness, pain, clumsiness or loss of balance. Lack of mobility is not only significant because it deprives us of our freedom of movement but its loss will lead to dependency.

Arthritis

Arthritis is by far the most common reason for impaired mobility. By the time we reach old age most people will have some evidence of osteoarthritis* in some of their major joints. The cause of this condition (in common with most forms of arthritis) is unknown. Its name suggests that it is secondary to infection but there is no confirmatory evidence to support this view. Such a theory about osteoarthritis has been both in and out of fashion at various times during this century. Currently the weight of evidence is again beginning to swing in a positive direction. There is, however, no doubt that the constant trauma to the joints plays an important role in causation. This probably accounts for the increasing incidence with increasing age — reflecting the unavoidable damage that is inflicted on our joints during a long and active life. People who have exposed individual joints to particularly excessive wear and tear throughout life are the most likely to develop pathological changes of osteoarthritis*. Essentially the condition is due to the destruction of the cartilage layer which covers the ends of the bones, where they articulate with each other. Without this covering, the friction involved with each movement increases — the joint becomes less efficient and movement becomes painful and sometimes noisy. Because of decreased use of the joint, its surrounding muscles become weaker and are less able to move and support the joint. In the late stages, extra bony development may appear at the edge of the joint and the surrounding muscles become stiff and fibrotic, hence hindering even more the normal action of the joint.

It is the largest joints which are most likely to suffer from these changes – especially the hips and knees. The spine is also frequently involved. In the early stages of the disorder, pain-relieving tablets will be sufficient to enable continued use of the joints. Extra strengthening may be gained by activity, or specific exercises for the joints. The special skills of a physiotherapist will be invaluable in planning such courses of treatment. If the joint changes progress to such an extent that normal activities (including sport) become impossible, then referral to an orthopaedic surgeon is needed for consideration of joint replacement. Combined metal and plastic joints inserted into the hip have been one of the most successful developments of modern surgery and have truly prolonged active life for many patients. Unfortunately the new joints do not last as long as nature's originals and a further replacement may be needed after ten years of use.

Rheumatoid arthritis

Rheumatoid arthritis is less common but in its more severe form it has a tendency to be more crippling than other forms of arthritic pathology. It can affect any joint, but involvement of the joints of the arms and hands make it very effective in stripping a patient of their independence. In this condition the joint-lining membrane goes berserk and rapidly overgrows, extending into and destroying the surrounding bone, the joints thus being totally destroyed. This disease may arise at any time of life, from childhood to old age. However, the elderly will account for many cases as there are at the end of life – those who have struggled with the disease for many years – and new cases arising in old age. Initially treatment concentrates on suppressing pain and the proliferation of the lining membrane. Physiotherapy will attempt to preserve maximum function, surgical intervention can sometimes replace deformed joints and minimize the handicap caused by others. More potent forms of treatment, such as steroids, gold and penicillamine, are used in severe forms only as the side-effects of these preparations can be severe.

Gout

Of all the arthritic conditions, this is traditionally that most associated with ageing. The caricature of the debauched old man, with an excessively painful foot and an enlarged big toe, and short temper, is well-known. However, frugal living will not automatically protect from this very painful disorder. The joints become painful because of irritation caused in the joint cavity by the precipitation of small crystals of uric acid. Primarily it is the handling of uric acid that is at fault and this can now be modified by the regular taking of a drug known as Zyloric (a xanthine oxidase inhibitor). Although the joint symptoms are likely to draw the victim's attention to the problem, it is in fact the quieter silting up of the kidney by similar crystals that may occasionally be life-threatening.

Pseudogout is a very similar condition, where again crystals form in joints, but the mechanism is entirely unknown. The only treatment available is therefore that of symptomatic relief, so analgesics with anti-irritation properties are used to suppress pain.

Nervous system

Strokes

In a British population of a quarter of a million people, and on an average day, about two people will suffer a stroke. Three-quarters of these victims will be of pensionable age. About half of those affected will die during the month following their first episode. The survival of the remainder will vary considerably in both quality and quantity. Some will make a complete recovery and live a normal lifespan*; others may become totally dependent.

A stroke results from an area of brain being starved of oxygen and nutrients. The affected area dies and shrinks to form a scar. The part of the body that was previously controlled by that damaged region will no longer function satisfactorily although compensation can occur by other areas taking over the activity.

The most familiar appearance after a stroke is of a patient paralysed down one side and with the face drawn across the opposite side. Speech may be lost or impaired and sight on the side of the weakness may be lost. In severe cases the patient may be unconscious and breathing laboured.

The blood supply that nurtures the brain can be interrupted by a bleed (cerebral haemorrhage) or a blockage in a blood-vessel (cerebral thrombosis). Both types of disorder tend to occur suddenly and unexpectedly and the term *cerebrovascular accident* is used to describe the illness. Sometimes the interference with the brain's blood supply is only temporary – in which case the symptoms of loss or impairment of function are transient. These episodes (transient ischaemic attacks) are important as they may frequently be due to abnormalities outside the brain which have interrupted the brain's blood flow. Small clots breaking off from a heart valve or changes in the performance of the heart are possibilities. Their great importance is that they can more often be corrected than other causes of stroke. A search for such an underlying cause must therefore be made. Any 'little stroke' which may present with interference in vision, difficulty in speech, unexpected falls, or transient weaknesses should always be reported to the doctor. A treatable cause may be found and more severe and permanent episodes may be prevented. Hopefully, in the long term it may be possible to reduce the incidence of strokes by controlling factors which tend to damage blood vessels – for example, smoking, excessively fatty diets and high blood pressure.

Recovering from a stroke. The road to recovery from a stroke can be very long and ardous. Many years of work and perseverance may be required from the victim, his relatives and friends and a whole band of skilled therapists. It is likely that the patient's life will never return to its previous normality. This is not to say that recovery of independence is not possible, but some disability is likely to remain which will alter the patient's lifestyle.

At the outset of the illness, admission to hospital is likely to be needed if the stroke appears to be life-threatening, but with the possibility of survival, and also if there is some doubt as to the precise nature of the attack (Table 10). Once the acute and diagnostic problems have been resolved, the period of rehabilitation has begun. The severity

Table 10 *Age and outcome of patients admitted to hospital with a stroke*

Age	Discharged from hospital (%)	Remaining in hospital (%)	Death (%)
Under 65	80	12	8
65–74	50	27	23
Over 75	40	20	40

of the residual disabilities and the amount of available support at home will decide whether some, all or none of this period of activity needs to be spent in hospital. If rehabilitation takes place from home the geriatric day hospital can play an important role in the programme. The skills of doctors, nurses, physiotherapists, occupational therapists, speech therapists and social workers may all be required, and they will treat and train not only the patient but also his helpers. The stroke victim's accommodation may also need to be modified or even completely changed. Life is rarely the same after a stroke (Table 11).

Table 11 *Functional recovery from stroke*

Upper limb	%
No movement	13
Some movement, no function	49
Some function	27
Full function	11
Lower limb	
Confined to wheelchair	19
Requiring wheelchair out of doors	11
Walking adequately	34
Walking normally	36

Parksinson's disease

Parkinson's disease has recently become increasingly important — not just because of increasing public awareness but because of new information about its cause and treatment. Developments from this new knowledge have far-reaching possibilities which may help us to influence other degenerative conditions of the nervous system.

Patient's with Parkinson's disease have difficulty in carrying out simple movement, or starting actions; they are stiff, and their limbs may also shake, resulting in slowness and clumsiness. Both fine movements (dressing) and coarse movements like walking become difficult. Accidents due to falls and dropping things become more common.

In Parkinson's disease the problem lies in the gap between the cells which make up the nerves in the brain. The messages in the nerves need to jump across the gap for the desired function to occur. The 'jump' is made by means of chemicals (neurotransmitters*) transferred from one nerve end to the other. In Parkinsons's disease the messenger is levodopa. It is now possible to supplement the amount of levodopa available to the nervous system and increase the effectiveness of the amount still present. Function can then be returned towards normality. Unfortunately the underlying degenerative process continues so that a stage can still be reached where the supplements remain insufficient. New treatments have greatly increased the quality and quantity of life available to sufferers from Parkinson's disease. Unfortunately they are not a cure, however, but a delaying process.

Physiotherapists, occupational therapists and speech therapists, also have much to offer in the mangement of this disease, and help should also be sought from the Parkinson's Disease Society (see appendix). This self-help group does much good work in supporting the victims of the disorder and their helpers, and it also generates interest and finance for further research into new developments.

Motor neurone disease

This is a progressive disorder of muscles, which becomes most common after the age of 50. The affected muscles melt away and can sometimes be seen to quiver under the skin. Any muscles may be affected but those of the legs, hands, tongue, and throat are most vulnerable. The condition is painless and mental function remains intact; bladder and bowels are under perfect control. If the legs only are affected, the disease may progress for many years with little limitation of the quantity or quality of life, when the muscles of swallowing are involved (progressive bulbar palsy), the course of the disease is usually rapid and death soon occurs — usually due to pneumonia, as food spills over into the lungs and causes irritation and infection.

Mobility and immobility

Unfortunately the cause of this condition is unknown and there are currently no effective methods of treatment.

Bone disease

Osteoporosis

Everyone's bones change as they age, becoming thinner and more brittle. These changes (osteoporosis) are most marked in women as they achieve a smaller amount of bone in youth, they live longer and their bone loss suddenly accelerates at the time of the menopause. If these ageing bones only retained their previous strength, there would be no problem. Unfortunately they become more susceptible to damage and fracture easily. In the case of the spinal vertebrae this is most likely to make itself evident by the onset of backache. The pains are likely to fluctuate, symptoms easing as damaged bones repair themselves and then recurring at the time of further damage and crushing. These episodes of pain may in themselves be incapacitating but more serious interference with walking will be caused by a fracture of a major leg bone — thigh (femur) or hip bone (Table 12). Unfortunately this is common and becomes increasingly so as people age.

Table 12 *Fractured neck of thighbone (femur). Rate per 1000 population in same age group*

Age in years	Rate
<50	0.04
50–54	0.12
55–59	0.35
60–64	0.56
65–69	0.88
70–74	1.74
75–79	4.88
80–84	9.42
85–89	18.4
90–94	20.0
95+	25.0

Over half the beds in orthopaedic wards are occuped by patients over the age of 60, usually due to a fracture sustained often during a fall, but sometimes after minimal injury. Their broken and displaced bones need to be fixed quickly, and wherever necessary metal plates or pins are used. When the hip is involved, the entire hip is often replaced with a metal or plastic joint. Early operation is important as frail people are not fit enough to survive a long period of bedrest! They need to be remobilized quickly so that their independence is not lost and so that they may escape the many serious complications of immobility.

Osteomalacia

Up to one-quarter of elderly patients with fractures have an additional bone problem. Osteomalacia is the softening of bone which occurs in vitamin D deficiency. This is a painful condition and is associated with pain and weakness of the muscles around the hips. Even without the complication of a fracture, this condition can therefore impair walking ability. It is not clear why so many elderly people (perhaps as many as 10 per cent) develop this adult form of rickets. A diet poor in vitamin D (a fat-soluble vitamin found in fatty fish and dairy products) can be responsible; more important is lack of exposure to sunlight, which enables the skin to produce its own vitamin D. Defects in the handling of vitamin D by the liver and kidneys may also play an important role.

Although a difficult disease to diagnose, especially in its early stages, it is an important one for doctors to pursue. If detected it is easy to give vitamin D supplements, but as the treatment can be dangerous if overdone it must be managed with skill and constant observation with regular blood tests. If treated early some episodes of broken bones may be avoided.

Pagets's disease

Paget's disease is another bone condition which has particular preference for the elderly. It is most frequently found in the United Kingdom, United States, Australia, New Zealand, West Germany and France, and rarely in Scandinavia, Switzerland, Africa and the Far East. There are about three-quarters of a million sufferers in the United Kingdom, most of whom are asymptomatic and quite unaware of their potential problem. In Paget's disease there is a breakdown in the fine control of the process of normal continuous resorption and replacement of bone. As a result the affected areas of bones (especially the skull, pelvis and tibiae) becomes enlarged and distorted and may be painful. Although thickened the bones are weaker than usual and can easily fracture. Most serious of all (but rare) is the risk of the diseased areas becoming malignant. The enlarged bones may also cause trouble by exerting pressure on the nearby structures, especially nerves (for example, the nerves emerging from the spinal cord and skull).

The cause of Paget's disease of the bone is not definitely known. It is possible that the process may be triggered off by a virus. Patients whose only complaint is of pain are usually simply treated with analgesics. Those with more serious complications or resistant pain, should be treated with hormone injections of calcitonin, a substance produced in special areas of the thyroid gland. It is currently an expensive and complicated form of treatment and is not used routinely.

Malignant disease

The most severe and persistent form of bone pain is that due to malignant disease. The lesions are usually due to spread of a cancer arising elsewhere, such as the breast, lung, prostate or a blood disease (myeloma) akin to leukaemia. Dissemination to the skeleton is usually a late stage in these disorders and indicates that a cure is unlikely. Efforts are therefore directed to the relief of the symptoms, either by potent painkillers, or by the use of deep X-ray therapy. Some relief can also be gained in certain cases by the use of special hormone preparations.

Peripheral problems

Walking may be greatly hampered by diseases that affect the nerves, blood vessels, and skin of the lower limbs and feet.

When the blood supply to the muscles of the legs becomes impaired, initially all will be well. But when extra blood flow is required — for instance, on walking — the muscles will be inadequately supplied and pain will occur. This is known as *intermittant claudication* and is an early symptom of narrowing of the arteries in the lower limbs. Sometimes it can be due to a well-defined and isolated blockage which can be demonstrated with special X-rays. In such cases surgeons can remove or bypass the obstruction and normal function is restored. If the underlying disease is more widespread and the symptoms begin to significantly hamper normal activity, an alternative approach can be adopted. The tight grip that the nervous system has over the diameter of the vessels can be released by the performance of an operation or an injection around the origin of these nerves in the region of the spine. This procedure is known as a *sympathectomy* — after the name of that particular part of the nervous system. In some cases the reduced blood supply continues to worsen to such a degree that sections of the foot can no longer survive. The starved foot may become very painful, and eventually gangrene will set in; at this unfortunate stage, there is no alternative but amputation. After a period of training in the use of an artificial limb, the patient should then be able to return to leading an active and mobile life.

An intact nervous system which transmits messages both up and down the lower limbs is essential for normal function. It is not only touch which is important, but even of greater value is our sense of position, which enables us to walk and use our limbs without looking to check on their position. In the absence of this sensory information walking becomes very clumsy and dangerous. Lack of touch exposes the limbs to serious dangers which may lead to mutilating damage.

Elderly diabetic patients are especially vulnerable to damage to both their nerves and blood-vessels, and therefore account for the highest number of amputations of the lower limbs. Detailed care of their extremities and fine diabetic control will help them to avoid such disastrous consequences of their disease.

Foot care becomes increasingly important to all people as they age, as feet are generally less able to recover from insults. Attention to foot hygiene becomes more difficult because of possible visual impairment, and is also hindered by arthritic changes in the hands, spine and hips, which can complicate access to one's toes and toenails. Unfortunately painful and neglected feet are a serious handicap to walking. If self-care in this department becomes impossible, the help of a trained chiropodist is essential. They are sadly in short supply but treatment by untrained and unskilled practitioners must be avoided. Doctors, nurses or health visitors can recommend suitable staff, but as one may have to wait for treatment, it is vital to act promptly.

Mobility and immobility

Loss of balance

Our balancing skills tend to become impaired as we age. Although this can be demonstrated by detailed scientific experiment, it rarely progresses to the stage of interfering with normal living; it may be a feature that contributes to the high incidence of falls in old age, especially in women (see Table 13).

Further impairment of balance may occur due to the presence of disease processes. The inner ear is essential for keeping us on an even keel, and damage to this area is often associated with deafness and is unfortunately irreversible and unresponsive to drugs. Simple and common problems, such as waxy ears, are easily detected and corrected and should always be considered.

People with a generalized reduction in brain-blood flow may also complain of general unsteadiness and dizziness. When the lowest part of the brain (brain stem), or its blood supply via the vessels running alongside the spine in the neck, is affected by disease these symptoms become very common.

If the normal compensating mechanisms fail to correct a fall in blood pressure on standing, the subject will feel unsteady. In severe cases, he will actually fall to the ground — the blood pressure then rising. Such feeling of dizziness on standing — especially in a warm environment — are commonplace to us all. However, this becomes increasingly frequent with ageing. It is more exaggerated in those people suffering from neurological disorders which maintain the fine control on blood pressure levels. Diabetic patients are particularly at risk. Many drugs can also potentiate this ageing change; diuretics and many tranquillisers and antidepressants are particularly at fault and must be used with caution by some elderly patients. Dizziness and falls can become so frequent and severe that attempts at walking become dangerous and unsuccessful.

Falls

Falling over is always unpleasant and frightening. To fall frequently and unpredictably, without obvious cause, is terrifying. In such circumstances, all confidence is rapidly lost and the subject becomes virtually bed or chair-fast.

However, it is the physical trauma that causes most concern to those who suffer from falls. Clearly much damage can be sustained — from simple painful bruising to serious fractures and even death (Table 13).

Table 13 *Mortality statistics due to falls*

Age in years	Male	Female
15	59	47
15–24	145	29
25–34	93	22
35–44	82	36
45–54	123	50
55–64	161	112
65–74	249	340
75 over	712	2074
Total for 1981	1624	2710

Other less obvious consequences are likely to accrue from any period of forced immobility spent on a hard floor, sometimes in an inhospitable environment. It should not be forgotten that once down an elderly person's pathologies may prevent him or her from getting up without assistance. Pressure sores can be acquired in the very short space of a few hours, and they may take months to heal. If the temperature at the scene of the accident is low then hypothermia becomes a serious risk. Pneumonia due to impaired chest movement may proceed to life-threatening dimensions. Dehydration will also occur if the period before rescue is prolonged. Clearly all possible steps must be taken to prevent falls. Risks must be identified and eliminated if possible, or at least minimized.

12

Bladder control

Bladder control remains one of the unmentionables in polite society. It is acceptable that babies have difficulty in learning to control their bladder functions. Once mastery has been achieved, it is taken for granted until the risk of its loss is almost expected in the 'sans everything' stage of life.

Continence mechanisms

The mechanisms of continence are complex and depend upon physiological and anatomical normality of the bladder itself, its supporting structures and outlet (Table 14). Communications between the bladder

Table 14   *Urinary symptoms in 557 people over the age of 65 (from Geriatric Medicine for Students, by Brocklehurst and Hanley, published by Livingstone)*

	Male	Female	All
Nocturia	70	61	64
Precipitancy	28	32	30
Urgency	14	9	10
Difficulty	13	3	7
Scalding	7	13	11
Total incontinence	17	23	20
Stress incontinence	3	12	9

and the brain must be intact. Convenience and opportunity of voiding are also of great significance, and the chances of compromised function are consequently great. Bladder accidents therefore occur throughout life — far more frequently than is realized or even acknowledged. A survey amongst healthy young female students has recorded occasional accidents in as many as 50 per cent! Because of anatomical differences the problems are less severe in males but are equalized as life progresses.

Urination at night

The most common change in bladder habit on ageing is the increasing frequency of the need to get up at night to pass water. The majority of elderly people have their sleep disturbed in this way. The main reason is that the decreased efficiency of the kidneys (see Chapter 5 and 6) makes it impossible for them to cope with a normal water load during the day. the 'night shift' is therefore brought in to compensate. Avoiding a large fluid intake in the evening will help but total intake should not be restricted. There are far-reaching consequences from this need to urinate in the night. The bedroom should be kept warm; a toilet (or commode) must be nearby, with good lighting and a clear route to it.

Bladder disorders

Female problems

The short outlet (urethra) from the female bladder makes women particularly vulnerable to bladder disorders, its shortness also makes it more prone to ascending infection. Irritation due to sexual activity can increase the susceptibility to infection. Hormonal changes after the menopause also impair the resistance to contamination. Stretching due to previous pregnancy can distort the anatomy so that the usual supporting muscles of the pelvis lose their efficiency.

Prostate problems

Men are only likely to become aware of urinary problems when their prostate gland has reached a sufficient size to start to impair bladder emptying. The prostate is a gland which is situated at the base of the bladder and surrounds its outlet tract, it slowly enlarges throughout life and by middle age may begin to affect the passage of urine so that a 40-year-old man has a 10 per cent chance of requiring a prostatectomy before the age of 80. The most common symptoms are frequency of the desire to pass urine, inability to put off the need to empty the bladder, a reduction in the strength of stream of urine and then persistent dribbling once the bladder action has been completed. The symptoms of prostatic enlargement may continue for many years without any serious complications, and may, in fact, fluctuate considerably even resolving without any medical or surgical intervention. However, for some the closure of the bladder outlet by the enlarging prostate progresses continuously with increasing difficulty in emptying the bladder. Eventually voiding may become impossible, and retention of urine will occur; quite rapidly the patient becomes very uncomfortable and will seek medical help. The examining doctor will have no difficulty in coming to a diagnosis, as the enlarged bladder is easily felt on palpation of the abdomen.

Treatment. An examination of the rectum* usually reveals the enlarged prostate gland as responsible. Instant relief can be given by the insertion of a catheter (a fine tube) into the bladder via the penis. The discomfort of the procedure is minimized by the use of a lubricant and a local anaesthetic. The immediate easing of the pain from the overdistended bladder produces immensely grateful patients. Once the bladder is draining successfully through the catheter the patient will need to undergo an operation to trim the prostate gland down to size, and this is most conveniently carried out by the same route as the catheter. The laboratory examination of the pieces of gland removed can then decide whether the excess growth is due to a malignant (cancerous) or benign condition, and this will influence the course of subsequent treatment.

An operation is not always necessary, nor always possible. The episode of obstruction may have been precipitated by the bladder being placed under abnormal stress. In such cases a recurrence can be prevented after the catheter has been removed by taking care in the future to avoid the triggering insult. Some risk factors are

(1) the injudicious use of potent diuretics;*

(2) an excessive intake of fluid during a short period, as may occur during celebratory alcohol consumption, for instance;

(3) the voluntary delay in bladder emptying due to social factors, such as a prolonged journey without access to toilet facilities;

(4) the provocative side-effects of some medications, for example, some antiasthma preparations or antidepressants.

In the minority of patients surgical intervention may be necessary but inadvisable because of general frailty, so here a permanent catheter will be needed. With regular changing, hygiene techniques and a good fluid intake, it should not be necessary to make any other significant change to the patient's lifestyle.

Polyuria

The passing of large and frequent amounts of urine is a very inconvenient symptom which may indicate the presence of an underlying illness. Most commonly it is due to treatment taken to counteract excess fluid retention, as in some forms of heart disease. However, the inconvenience caused by such diuretics* can be minimized if care is taken to match patient needs and drug action. Some diuretics* act very rapidly and cause copious urine to be passed within a few hours. Others have a more prolonged and gentle action, lasting more than 12 hours. It is therefore important that both patient and doctor discuss what is needed to ensure that the maximum beneficial effects are achieved without total destruction of the patient's normal pattern of life. Some patients prefer to shift their fluid rapidly, first thing in the morning or last thing at night. However, good mobility is essential in order to respond to the sudden urge. Others who are slower on their feet opt for a more controlled effect — but care is needed to ensure that the task is over before bedtime in order to avoid unnecessary interference with sleep. Special attention may be needed to avoid inconvenient timing with social activities such as shopping and visiting.

Excess urine flow can be caused by the body's need to excrete abnormally high levels of substances. Sugar is the most frequently encountered example. People with high levels of sugar in their blood are diabetic, and the system tries to correct the blood by washing the sugar away in urine rather than storing it in the body in the normal way. An increase in the frequency of urination may therefore be one of the first symptoms of diabetes. People with failing kidneys may also present with these symptoms, their kidneys acting as leaky sieves rather than efficient conservers of salt and other vital substances.

Painful micturition

If the passage of urine becomes painful (dysuria) the most likely explanation is an infection. The pain may be associated with other symptoms such as sudden desire to urinate and increased frequency. Infections of the bladder may occur in isolation but if they are recurrent there is often another underlying problem, for instance partial obstruction, stones in the tract or destructive lesions such as a growth. Clearly each episode must be taken seriously — a clean specimen of urine will be needed for the laboratory to grow the bacteria responsible and indicate the most appropriate antibiotic. After recurrent episodes, the search must be made for any underlying cause.

Blood in the urine

Blood in the urine (haematuria) is a frightening symptom. If associated with pain it is probably a complication of a fairly severe infection or excess pressure due to an obstruction. If painless the inferences may be more sinister indicating the presence of a growth — but not necessarily a malignant and life-threatening one. These patients must see their general practitioner straightaway, and they may be referred to a specialist clinic.

Defective bladder control

Uncertainty about bladder function may have either a simple or serious explanation. In women, one of the most common causes is changes in the vaginal lining due to hormone lack following the menopause. Women with this condition may never be quite sure whether they do or do not want to empty their bladder. They usually play safe and find that they frequently pass water but only in small amounts, and they will also have false alarms when none is passed. A quick examination by a doctor will soon confirm the diagnosis and the problem will respond to hormone replacement therapy.

Unawareness of the bladder in a mentally competent person is a warning or underlying serious neurological disease. If sensation in the bladder is impaired it can slowly and painlessly fill until the natural barriers of the outlet are overcome and urine will then freely trickle out without any awareness. This disaster can happen in neurological conditions like multiple sclerosis or when the spinal cord has been damaged by a tumour or by an accident. Fortunately these conditions are rare in the elderly.

Intellectual failure is the most common cause of uncontrolled urination in old age. People with severe dementia (see Chapter 10) often have uninhibited and unstable bladders. The normal, learnt process of preventing bladder emptying — unless it is socially allowable — is lost as widespread damage affects the high centres of the brain. Normally suppressed minor contractions of the bladder are therefore allowed to progress to emptying. A sudden distraction can also more easily overcome the reduced powers of inhibition and urine can therefore be suddenly and unexpectedly voided. People with dementia are also at a considerable disadvantage in that they cannot plan to empty their bladder before finding themselves in the embarrassing position. They may then be literally caught out — with an urgent need to pass urine — but with no accessible toilet, or an inability to remember its location. The patient, fortunately, is usually unaware of any unsocial behaviour.

Treatment

Clearly many disturbances of bladder function can be corrected. For example, infections will respond to antibiotics, compensation can be made for hormonal deficiency states, abnormalities can be removed surgically, and weakened pelvis muscles can be surgically strengthened or supported by ring pessaries. However, these forms of treatment can only be initiated if the doctor is consulted and the correct diagnosis is made. It should never be assumed that any bladder change is simply the consequence of ageing and merely an inconvenience which must be hidden and tolerated. Unfortunately cures are not always possible but opportunities to offer help may remain. Where the defect in function cannot be corrected, it will still be possible to minimize the difficulties. The choice of method for managing such recalcitrant problems lie between catheterization or the use of protective padding; £36 million was spent on such measures in 1981.

Elastic sheath. In men it may be possible to manage the problem by using an elastic sheath. This can be applied to the penis and allow continuous drainage into a discreet bag worn on the leg. Unfortunately no such simple drainage apparatus has been designed for the use of women. Several attempts have been made but they all result in painful ulceration and damage to the vulva. Catheterization is the only mechanical solution available to women and men unable to wear a sheath.

Catheters. Where a catheter (a tube left in the bladder) is acceptable to a patient it probably offers the solution which allows the greatest freedom. Generally such a solution is only possible in patients with good insight into their problems and who are happy and able to assist in the maintenance of such a drainage programme. The catheter can be either blocked off and released at regular and convenient intervals, or allowed to drain continuously into a bag. The bag can be easily concealed under the patient's clothing and should be undetectable to others (both by eyes and noses). There are problems with the long-term use of catheters, especially the risk of recurrent infections; however, in such desperate circumstances, the advantages generally outweigh the potential problems.

Pads. The theory behind the various padding devices is that the urine should be absorbed into the pad preventing leakage. A waterproof layer is generally used to prevent outward spread of the urine and a fine non-absorbent layer is usually employed to separate the patient's skin from the wet pad. Special super-absorbent substances (sometimes a gel) are used in the pads so that a large volume of urine can be accommodated. By separating the skin from the pad it is hoped that skin irritation can be avoided. Special undergarments have been designed to hold these pads without leakage or slippage. The same principles are used in the manufacture of incontinence pads which may be used in bed or as seat covers. The advice of the doctor and nurse should always be taken before such an appliance is used, first to ensure that a reversible cause of the problem is not being overlooked, and second, so that appropriate garments are used if necessary. It is important that commonly used rubber pants and nappy-like garments should not be used. They are aesthically unacceptable, and more seriously, can frequently result in distressing damage to the skin.

Although urinary symptoms including incontinence become more common with increasing age, they should not be tolerated in silence. Most elderly people retain their continence and are able to lead normal and active lives in spite of any change in bladder habit. All health districts should be establishing a urinary continence advisory service.

13

Ears, eyes, teeth, skin, and hair

There are very few life-threatening conditions which affect these areas. Nevertheless, there is no doubt about their importance. Any impairment of the function of these organs exposes a person to dangers and strips life of much of its pleasure (Fig. 7).

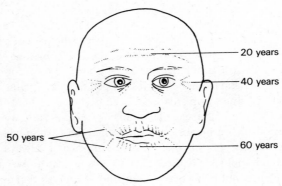

Fig. 7. The ageing face.

Ears

Everybody knows that our ears are for hearing — but in addition they have the function of maintaining equilibrium. Ability to hear acutely tends to decline with age (a process known as presbycusis) and begins at the age of 30 years. The perception of high-pitched sounds is most affected. Differentiation between sounds is also impaired — this is an important loss in noisy surroundings — and in such circumstances it may be difficult to follow one conversation among many others. Perhaps this is one reason why overcrowded cocktail parties are more favoured by 'bright young things' than by mature sages!

The wax in our ears also changes with age, becoming harder and less likely to clear itself spontaneously from the outer ear. As it accumulates it may form a very hard plug which will effectively impair the transmission of sound waves down to the ear drum and onwards. When these two ageing phenomena occur together there can be very significant hearing loss.

It is therefore not surprising that deafness is common in old age. We do not really know how many people are affected but it has been estimated to be one-third of those over 65, rising to half over 80 years of age. Unfortunately many accept it as a normal part of old age, and therefore do not seek help and remain handicapped, usually unnecessarily. About one-eighth of a million people over 65 years of age are registered as having impaired hearing. This is certainly only the tip of the iceberg, but they are probably the most severely affected.

Advice should be sought as the majority can be helped. Wax is easily identified by a doctor and can be painlessly syringed away after an initial period of softening with regular drops. Presbycusis can be overcome by the fitting of a hearing aid but this must be properly maintained. Operations to free the internal mechanisms of the ear can also be performed when indicated. Patients needing such help often have a family history of deafness and will have themselves been afflicted probably in early middle age. Otosclerosis is the most common diagnosis in these circumstances, where articulating bones in the inside of the ear have become fused and need to be released so that they can more effectively transmit sound waves. These internal mechanisms can also become damaged during ear and throat infections, and surgical intervention may be required. Hearing aids are often very effective in minimizing any residual defects.

Some drugs — especially antibiotics of the streptomycin or gentamycin type — are liable to damage hearing if given in excessive doses. The elderly are particular vulnerable in this respect and great care is needed in the use of these drugs in old age.

Helping people with deafness

The first stage is trying to understand their problems. Because they cannot hear properly does not mean that they live in silence. Usually they are constantly distracted by additional or distorted sounds. They feel very isolated, sometimes to the extent of being precipitated into mental illness. Both depression and paranoia* are frequent problems in the deaf. The uncertainty about auditory contact increasing the risk of suspicion and doubt about the intentions and aims of associates.

Communication is made easier if the person talking speaks clearly and slowly. He should position himself so that the available light shines on his face not from behind him. He should not obscure his mouth with a cigarette, pencil etc, or turn away when talking. All extraneous noises and distractions should be abolished wherever possible.

Hearing aids. A deaf person should not hesitate to inform a new acquaintance of his or her difficulty and to give advice about overcoming the problem. When there is concern about failing hearing, medical advice should be taken. Once initial difficulties like wax have been excluded, the patient's suitability for a hearing aid will be considered. However, it should not be expected that an appliance will restore hearing to normal. The volume of received speech will be increased but distortions and extra noises will remain a problem. Special facilities can be provided to supplement a hearing aid: many public places, such as theatres, have installed a loop system which improves reception to an aid; British Telecom can fit an inductive coupler to telephones, an apparatus which helps to eliminate background noise when a hearing aid is used. It is national policy for this adaptation to be installed in all public call boxes, and those currently altered can be identified by the World Deaf symbol. To benefit from this system it is necessary to have one of the new postaural hearing aids which incorporate a three-position switch. British Telecom also offer other forms of help to telephone users, such as additional ear pieces so that both ears may be used, loudspeakers, volume controls for the telephone bell (or its replacement by a flashing light). The local telephone sales office can supply further information.

Eyes

Blindness

Blindness may start as intermittent or permanent loss of vision. The permanent forms may come on suddenly or gradually. It is the transient episodes and gradual deterioration which are of greatest importance, as they have a greater chance of successful intervention and prevention of serious permanent impairment.

Intermittent blindness. Most fleeting episodes of blindness are due to abnormalities in the blood supply to the retina (light-sensitive part of the eye) or to the part of the brain which receives and interprets messages (the occipital region at the back of the brain) or the connecting pathways. A reduction in blood flow may result from an alteration in the effectiveness of the circulation; a fall in blood pressure, or an alteration in the rate or rhythm of the heart may be responsible. The partial obstruction of a blood vessel may occur due to the passage of a small clot (embolus); this may arise from a damaged heart valve or roughened area on the wall of the heart or an artery. Thickened blood vessels in the eye are also more vulnerable as the consequently narrowed lumen is more easily blocked. This can happen in patients with arteritis, an inflammatory thickening of the artery wall. However, all these conditions can be treated if detected. The brief loss of vision is therefore an important warning sign, which if ignored may allow the underlying changes to progress to permanent blindness. It is therefore essential that such symptoms are reported to your doctor so that attempts can be made to identify precipitating problems, which hopefully can then be reversed before serious damage occurs.

Several of the slowly progressive causes of blindness can be corrected or checked. The difficulty in their management is lack of awareness of the problem. It is amazing how restricted a person's vision can become before the problem is appreciated; this is particularly true where it is the scope of vision (visual field) which has gradually shrunk.

Glaucoma

Chronic glaucoma is the best example. In this condition the pressure in the eye gradually increases and results in damage to the optic nerve. As the process progresses, the angle of vision becomes increasingly narrow, until the victim is virtually looking down a narrow tunnel (Fig. 8). Because details in that tunnel are clearly and precisely seen the patient can manage to lead a surprisingly normal life, until a critical point of visual loss has been passed when it is then too late to regain the lost abilities. Early signs of the problem are really non-existent. Ten per

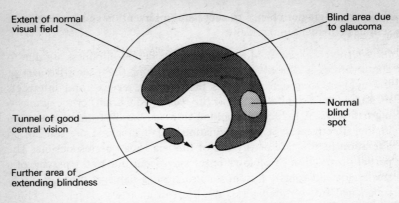

Fig. 8. Visual field of the right eye in a patient with glaucoma, progressing to complete tunnel vision.

cent of victims another member of the family will be affected. The only method of protection is regular eye testing, including the measurement of eyeball pressures. Treatment in early cases concentrates on reducing the eye pressure by instilling drops which either help the drainage of the fluid from the eye (pilocarpine) or reduce the production of fluid (Diamox or timolol). In the latter stages, relief can only be obtained by a surgical operation to enable free flow and drainage of fluid inside the eye; a small cut in the iris is the usual technique.

There is also an acute form of glaucoma, and this is a dramatic medical emergency. The patient becomes acutely ill with headache, vomiting and blurring of vision. The eye will appear red and angry. If the pressure is not relieved urgently in these eyes, then rapid blindness will result.

Cataract

A very common eye change in old age is cataract. This is a clouding of the lens which prevents light reaching the sensitive retina in the normal way. The condition accounts for about one-eighth of all ophthalmic outpatient appointments and half the department's operations. Although the condition is rare before old age, it can occur especially in vulnerable groups like diabetics. Most patients are over 70 years of age. Once formed the opacity persists and progresses and may eventually require

114

removal. Much skill is required in deciding when the opaque lens should be extracted. Postoperatively there are likely to be problems with adjustment to the new situation. Replacement lenses in the form of glasses cause considerable distortion of vision; this must be compensated for by the patient and is especially difficult if good vision remains in the unoperated eye. Contact lenses and lenses inserted into the eye give better vision but have acceptance and tolerance problems as far as the patient is concerned. When to operate is clearly a matter for careful discussion between surgeon and patient and so is the question of local or general anaesthesia. Age alone is never a contraindication to surgery and the duration of hospital stay will probably be between three and eight days.

Some alleviation of poor vision can be obtained without operation and before the cataract becomes very advanced. Spectacles or magnifying glasses may be helpful. Tinted glasses for shading of the eyes may overcome the problem of glare, and improved illumination for reading and close work will also be beneficial. Dilatation of the pupil with eye drops can also be helpful in some cases.

Destruction of the retina

Destruction of the light-sensitive retina is the third progressive form of blindness. To some extent atrophic ageing changes occur in this region in all elderly people. The back of the eye in old age — when seen through an ophthalmoscope — is paler than in youth. It tends to have a less abundant blood supply and extra amounts of pigment are to be seen scattered around the retina. Patients with long-standing or poorly controlled diabetes or high blood pressure are at extra risk. Bleeding into the eye and the development of new blood vessels are further complications which can seriously damage vision. Diabetes is now the most common cause of blindness in this country — either resulting from cataract formation or the destruction of the retina, or both together. The new blood vessel formation in diabetic eyes can be modified by laser treatment, and the same technique can be used in patients where the retina has become torn and detached; the laser burns are used in a controlled way to prevent further damage.

Eye tests

It is normal for visual acuity to deteriorate with increasing age (see

Chapter 6). It is therefore essential that the elderly arrange to have their eyes tested at regular intervals, thus ensuring that they always have the most suitable lenses in their glasses. Patients with diabetes, high blood pressure, and a family history of glaucoma must especially ensure that they receive routine examinations of their eyes and vision. Simple measures such as good lighting and clean spectacles or magnifying glasses should always be available.

Teeth

In old age the main problem is lack of teeth. This is most unfortunate as careful maintenance of preventive measures should enable people to retain their own teeth to the end of life. It is interesting that in wild animals it is loss of teeth through decay that leads to death through malnutrition and starvation. Fortunately such a drastic outcome is avoided in humans. Most teeth are lost as a result as a complication of periodontal (gum) disease; chronic infection and retraction of the gums will leave the teeth loose and insecure. It is an advantage if only a few teeth survive, so full-scale clearance should be avoided wherever possible. Any remaining teeth act as useful anchors for dental appliances, so a more snug and secure fit is therefore likely to be obtained.

Dentures

Dentures may themselves cause many problems. Irritation due to roughness or poor fitting can lead to severe persistent ulceration of the lining of the mouth. Poor occlusion of dentures can cause excess stresses and strains in the jaw and lead to painful arthritis of the temperomandibular joint. Poor fitting can lead to collapse of the mouth with poor sealing of the lips, so that saliva may escape at the corners, and lead to areas of maceration and fungal infection at that site. It should be remembered that the mouth continues to change shape after dental extraction; in particular the bone ridges recede, so dentures may therefore become loose and need regular replacement. Lack of natural teeth does not mean that one no longer needs to attend the dentist! If there are difficulties in visiting the dentist, it may be possible to use a domiciliary service for home attendance, or a mobile unit may be available. If such facilities are needed, contact should be made with the district health

116

authority's dental officer. Charges for dental treatment may present considerable difficulties, treatment is only free to the elderly if they are receiving supplementary benefits, in other words having savings of less than £2500. However, six-monthly checkups, repairs to dentures, and emergency treatment are all free. The total maximum costs should not be greater than £90, whatever treatment is needed.

Skin

The skin in older people has a slower cell turnover. The cells are smaller in size and number; the results of these changes are thinner and drier skin, and the supporting tissues in the skin are also reduced in amount. Increased laxity in skin shows itself as wrinkles. The horizontal furrows across the forehead are the first to appear after the age of 20 years. Next are crow's feet at 40 years, then wrinkles around the corner of the mouth from 50 years, and ten years later creases around the lips. This timing has considerable individual variation as extra exposure to sunlight and weather generally tends to precipitate these changes.

Another consequence of the reduction of supporting tissue in the skin is the appearance of spontaneous areas of bleeding, below the surface. These too are most likely to appear on exposed surfaces, especially the forearms. They are quite harmless, insignificant and painless.

Ageing skin also becomes drier and more scaly. These changes alone may be sufficient to account for the common complaint of generalized itching. Other causes, such as kidney failure, liver failure, severe iron deficiency anaemia, and endocrine disorders are much less common, and not specific to old age.

Spots, warts, and moles

Spots, warts, and moles all tend to increase in frequency in old age. Small cherry-red spots (macules) on the trunk — Campbell de Morgan spots — are common and harmless. Seborrhoeic warts (brown, disfiguring plaques) may become widespread, but these rather horny nodules are of no significance. Moles may be sinister especially if they bleed or rapidly increase in size, and help should be sought immediately. Similarly it is important not to ignore persistent ulcerated areas on the face. Both of these conditions may be malignant and may spread widely if not checked.

Diseases of the skin

There is little that is specific to the elderly concerning skin diseases. Psoriasis can affect any age group and the majority of sufferers take their disease into their old age. Eczema can also affect any age group, but the seborrhoeic forms due to changes in the oil glands in the skin often seem more severe and persistent in the elderly. Herpes zoster (shingles) can be very troublesome in old age. It is caused by the chicken-pox virus, and has usually been present since childhood. When resistance is low it may be roused and cause a very painful rash affecting either a segment of the body or one or the eyes and its surrounding skin. Anti-viral preparations are now available to shorten the course of the illness and its severity. The relief of pain and protection of sight (if the eye is affected) are the main functions of the supervising doctor.

Pemphigus is a life-threatening blistering condition which seems almost exclusively to affect the elderly. Fortunately it responds well to steroid treatment, which, however, is likely to be needed for the rest of the patient's life.

Drug reactions affecting the skin as rashes and itching are common in the elderly, mainly because they are the greatest users of medications.

Skin care

Skin care in old age should concentrate on cleanliness, but without excessive washing with potent soaps, etc. The skin should be kept moist with moisturizers. Exposure to trauma should be avoided wherever possible as healing may be slow. Prolonged and fierce sunshine should be considered as traumatic. Persistent and enlarging lesions are warnings and help and advice should be obtained.

Intertrigo. A particularly troublesome problem — especially in the obese and in hot conditions — is intertrigo. This consists of red, moist, sore smelly areas in skin folds, for example under the breasts or in the groin. Although lack of hygiene is responsible, some cases are resistant to washing as the skin may be infected with fungal organisms, and applying antifungal preparations to the skin is the only way of

118

clearing them. Vulval involvement can be the first sign of undiagnosed diabetes mellitus.

Leg ulcers

Leg ulcers become more frequent as people age, and are usually around the ankle region. In younger people they are nearly always a consequence of poor venous blood flow. The resulting statis leads to breakdown of the skin surface. Normally they are painless, unless the surrounding skin becomes infected. In older people there is likely to be an element of ischaemia due to narrowing of the arteries which supply that particular region; the subsequent oxygen lack may be the reason why these ulcers can be more frequently painful in older victims.

The main principles of treatment are regular cleaning of the ulcer and attempts to prevent local swelling. Although prolonged periods of rest can be beneficial in the young, such an approach may be counter-productive in the elderly. In some cases plastic surgery is the best solution to ensure rapid and complete healing. Unfortunately these ulcers may still persist as a chronic and unsightly burden, in spite of attempts at healing.

Hair

Hair becomes finer, greyer and less luxuriant as the years pass. The familiar male balding with receding forehead may also affect women if they live into their 80s and 90s. However, a general thinning of head hair is the most common hair change in elderly women. Body hair also declines and greys, and tends to be lost in the opposite order in which it was gained — trunk first, then legs, and finally pubic and axillary hair. It is very rare for anybody to live long enough to become totally hairless; conversely increased hairiness is likely to affect the facial appearance of elderly women to the extent that 40 per cent of those over the age of 80 are likely to be troubled by excessive facial hair. This may reach such proportions that regular shaving becomes necessary.

14

Nutrition and digestion

Intermittent symptoms from the digestive system are common throughout life, and are generally not of great significance. The magnitude of the inconvenience is not matched by serious consequences. However, during the ageing process abnormalities of the gut become increasingly frequent, and symptoms may therefore change and increase in importance. Perversely, some potentially dangerous abdominal conditions sometimes become asymptomatic in older people. In addition some bowel upsets are due to changes in other distant systems. Diagnostic problems in digestive upsets, therefore, become increasingly complex with ageing.

Loss of appetite and weight

Persistent loss of appetite and sudden weight loss must always be taken seriously. Usually they are non-specific markers of an underlying illness. Chronic ill-health due to longstanding heart failure, recurrent bronchitis or severe arthritis and many other conditions may be responsible. An occult growth or infection in any system can lead to weight loss. An upset in the endocrine glands, as for example in diabetes, or an overactive thyroid gland, can lead to dramatic weight reduction, but these are not usually associated with a poor appetite. The opposite may even occur (see Chapter 16).

Psychological disturbances — especially depression — can also significantly upset a patient's desire for food and the resultant reduced intake can lead to weight loss. Many medications can also impair appetite.

Because weight loss and appetite changes are such ubiquitous complaints, it is the associated symptoms that act as clues to the site of the precipitating cause. Nausea, vomiting, abdominal pain and changes in bowel habit are all concurrent problems that may indicate a potential gastrointestinal abnnormality.

Nutrition and digestion

Nausea and vomiting

These symptoms are not exclusive to disorders of the digestive system. They can also occur in some neurological conditions, especially where the inner ear and its balance functions are impaired, or where pressure inside the skull becomes raised. Endogenous poisoning due to the accumulation of excess waste products, such as occurs in kidney failure, may also be responsible.

When some of the pattern of symptoms are caused by disorders in the gastrointestinal tract the precipitating abnormality will usually be found in the upper part, such as the oeosphagus (gullet), stomach, duodenum, gallbladder and its ducts.

A transient, sudden and unexpected episode of vomiting is usually due to gastritis (irritation of the stomach lining). The stomachs of elderly people are more vulnerable because they are less likely to be protected from insult by a normal acid secretion. Acid production gradually declines with increasing age due to atrophy (degenerative changes) in the stomach lining. The acid has several functions but one is to protect the bowel from foreign invaders such as bacteria. These episodes of gastritis are usually self-limiting, and if allowed to rest the gut recovers spontaneously. Problems only arise if the illness is prolonged, and dehydration can then occur, but small amounts of water should be taken frequently to avoid complications.

In the oesophagus the two most likely problems are obstruction and irritation. When obstruction occurs, food becomes difficult to swallow, and can be felt to stick behind the breastbone, and may be regurgitated or vomited. When irritation is the main problem, the vomiting is likely to be associated with pain — particularly heartburn, where acid can be felt rising up into the throat. This sensation is, in fact, usually due to acid being allowed to rise up out of the stomach and hence irritate the sensitive lining of the gullet. A defect at the junction of the oesophagus and stomach is the usual cause and this is called a hiatus hernia.*

Both of these symptom complexes — regurgitation and food that sticks, and vomiting with heartburn — normally need to be investigated. The technique used in the first instance is a barium swallow, where in

121

this test the patient swallows a radio-opaque substance and its progress down the gullet can be observed on X-rays. Thus the site of the abnormality can nearly always be identified without difficulty, although there may be problems in establishing its nature for certain. Where there is doubt it will be necessary to arrange for the lesion to be seen directly; this can be done with the use of a narrow flexible telescope (fibroptic endoscope), and even more usefully a small piece can be removed by the instrument. Close microscopic examination can then be undertaken and the precise nature of the problem determined. This course of action is necessary when it is feared that an obstructing lesion is due to a cancerous growth. When such a serious diagnosis has been confirmed, its treatment will depend on the exact site and extent of the growth, the choice lying between radiotherapy to shrink the growth, its removal by surgery, or a bypass by a surgically inserted tube. Simple benign obstructions can sometimes be easily stretched — although this procedure may need to be repeated at regular intervals.

A hiatus hernia is an inconvenient defect but rarely serious, and surgical intervention to correct it is rarely required. Much symptomatic improvement can be obtained by simple measures such as weight loss — where there is obesity — avoidance of stooping and straining, and the regular use of preparations to neutralize or reduce acid secretions. A hiatus hernia is found in about 60 per cent of all people over the age of 60 years, and most of these (three-quarters) do get some symptoms (usually heartburn).

Indigestion

Indigestion implies pain or discomfort associated with eating. It is a very vague but common symptom. Throughout life, about one-third of people experience such problems, and in old age it rises to over a half. Most people become familiar with their own particular problems and they adapt their diet and lifestyle to minimize their distress, while maximizing their pleasures. Only if their symptoms change in nature or severity are they likely to seek medical help. The most common cause of indigestion in late life is a hiatus hernia* (see above).

Nutrition and digestion

Peptic ulceration and malignancy

Peptic ulceration of the stomach or duodenum is the next most frequent problem (Fig. 9). In both conditions the lining of the stomach or duodenum will have become eroded, either because of excess acid activity

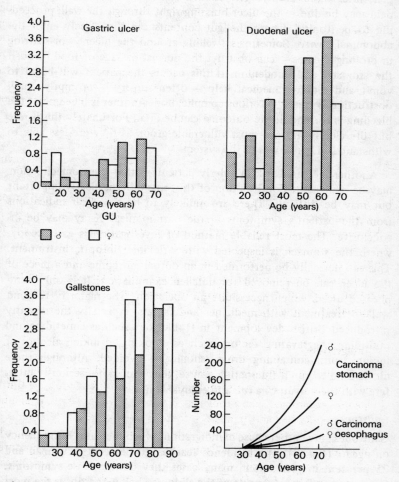

Fig. 9. Age distribution of some common digestive disorders.

or because of reduced resistance of the lining to normal wear and tear. Pain, of a boring nature, is usually situated in the upper part of the abdomen, and may either be precipitated or relieved by eating. In severe cases the pain may move through into the back as the ulcer penetrates more deeply. The sudden and dramatic worsening of the pain may be due to the ulcer bursting right through the wall, proceeding to peritonitis, where the gut contents can then freely enter the abdominal cavity. Sometimes swelling around the ulcer — or scarring in prolonged cases — can obstruct the normal passage of food through the stomach and duodenum. If this occurs the patient will begin to vomit and requires medical help — often surgery — promptly. Such obstruction is clearly a serious complication. Another is bleeding; if the bleeding is torrential, the outcome can be fatal. Fortunately this is rare but the elderly are the most vulnerable group as they are less able to withstand sudden shocks to the system.

Another increased risk in elderly patients is that the stomach lesion may be malignant. Confirmation of this possibility is clearly important but may be difficult. There are unlikely to be any clear indications from the patient's symptoms — the barium meal X-ray may be inconclusive. The most reliable method of investigation is gastroscopy, where the stomach is inspected with a flexible fibroptic instrument. This can normally be performed in an outpatient clinic and a piece of the ulcer can be removed for detailed examination. It is only complicated ulcers which necessitate an operation. The majority respond well to treatment with medicines and tablets, especially the recently introduced British development in H_2-blockers such as cimetidine and ranitidine. Aggravating factors such as smoking, drinking alcohol or taking aspirin-containing drugs, should be avoided. Although these ulcers tend to run a fluctuating course, they should not seriously interfere with the pursuit of a full and enjoyable life.

Gallstones

Gallstones are another cause of indigestion, which increases in frequency on ageing (Fig. 9). The incidence reaches 30 per cent in woman and 25 per cent in men but in many cases they do not cause symptoms. Sharp pains on the right side of the abdomen below the ribs is the most common way in which gallstones can advertise their presence, and these pains may become very severe and require painkillers. The constant irritation by the stone may cause the gallbladder to become inflammed and tender. The stone may escape from the gallbladder but lodge in the duct on its way into the bowel. As well as being painful, this may also lead to jaundice as the main exit from the liver may become blocked. The patient's skin becomes increasingly yellow as the jaundice and blockage progress. The correct diagnosis may be made on X-ray examination (cholecystogram) or ultrasound techniques (using reflections of sound waves to reveal the stones). When symptoms are severe there is no alternative to surgical removal of the stones. In some mild cases, with special types of stones, it can be possible to dissolve them away with tablets (chenodeoxycholic acid), but this takes several months. Painless jaundice may occur as a side-effect of some drugs (tranquillisers) and secondary to pancreatic* cancer.

Constipation

Many elderly people worry unnecessarily about their bowels. It should be appreciated that not everybody has their bowels open each day — the actual frequency of bowel clearance is not important, but regularity is. For some people it is normal for their bowels to move only on every third day, and for others alternate days or a similar pattern. There should only be concern if the pattern changes or the motions become difficult to pass. Small hard motions are the most difficult to evacuate. Poor dietary habits are the most frequent cause of constipation, and the simplest method of correction is to increase the amount of fibrous bulk in the food; fruit, vegetables (especially beans) and bran and wholemeal bread and flour are items in the diet which need to be increased.

Causes. Constipation can occur as a side-effect of many drugs. Analgesics (especially codeine derivatives), antidepressants and the older antiparkinsonian drugs are particuarly guilty. The abuse of violent purgatives during a long life can leave the bowel exhausted, flabby and unable to work properly. Imbalance of the body's chemistry and glands can also lead to constipation. High calcium levels due to hyperactivity of the parathyroid gland is a rare but significant cause.

Under activity of the thyroid gland (myxoedema) is a more common cause of constipation but once identified is easily corrected.

Constipation can be an early presenting symptom of obstruction of the lower bowel. It is for this reason that it must be taken seriously if it arises as a new symptom in later life. The necessary investigations (sigmoidoscopy and barium enema examinations) are simple and the surgical removal of an obstructing growth will be successful if no unnecessary delay has been allowed to occur (see below).

Laxatives. If help is required to ensure comfortable bowel evacuation a natural form of assistance is preferable. Simply increasing the bulk of the stools is often sufficient to resolve the problem of constipation, and this may be achieved by taking a diet with increased amounts of fibre (such as bran, wholemeal bread, extra fruit and vegetables). Bulking preparations are also available — Celevac, Isogel, Fybogel — which act by absorbing water when in the large bowel and thus increase the amount of residue to be excreted.

Stool softeners — such as dioctyl and Dorbanex are also safe and effective; the latter also contains a small amount of gut stimulant. Preparations containing irritants such as phenolphthalein are best avoided, and lubricating substances such as liquid paraffin also have many undesirable side-effects so cannot be recommended.

Haemorrhoids

Piles are dilated veins around the anus — just inside the body but if extensive they may enlarge downwards and hang below the anus. They are the result of increased pelvic pressures, usually secondary to constipation. The raised pressure interferes with normal blood flow and the veins become chronically engorged; problems arise when they bleed as the patient may become severely anaemic. Thrombosis in a pile will cause local pain. Localized itching (pruritus) and general irritation may also occur, frequently due to fungal infection of the protruding moist lesions. When symptomatic the piles may be removed by a simple surgical procedure; milder cases may be successfully treated by injections which cause shrinkage of the dilated veins.

Diarrhoea

An isolated episode of loose motions is no more significant in old age than in earlier life. It is only in infants and small children that serious sequelae are likely to arise. A brief self-limiting infection is usually found to be the cause. Simple measures concerning personal hygiene and a light liquid diet are all that are required to enable the bowel to make a spontaneous recovery.

Chronic inflammatory conditions are the most likely cause for prolonged diarrhoea in older people. The most common is diverticular disease, where pouches arising from the large bowel become inflamed and irritated, pain and diarrhoea are then likely to occur. These pouches occur in the majority of the elderly in the western world, and probably result from excess pressures in the bowel generated by the force needed to expel small, hard motions. Improving the consistency of the stools is the best method of treatment and prevention.

Inflammatory conditions such as Crohn's disease and ulcerative colitis are usually asociated with younger patients, but both illnesses can also occur towards the end of life. Impaired bowel function due to reduction in its blood supply is another cause of diarrhoea, and one almost exclusive to the elderly. Episodes of diarrhoea and abdominal pain are most likely to occur after eating, and the patient will have difficulty in maintaining his normal weight.

Activity at the upper end of the gut may also result in diarrhoea, dietary excesses of unaccustomed food and alcohol being the most common culprits. Medicines are also fairly frequently responsible, especially antibiotics, and excessive doses of digoxin and the abuse of purgatives are other examples. Anxiety can be another potent cause.

Faecal incontinence

Faecal incontinence is a disaster for both the patient and his immediate supporters. However, if the patient is aware of the problem it is likely that a treatable cause will be found. If the problem has an incurable cause, it will at least be possible for such a patient to cooperate with his carers so that the inconvenience and distress are minimized. In such circumstances a method of management can be devised which retains some degree of predictability concerning the patient's bowel habits.

The most difficult patients to look after are those who have no insight into their bowel problem, usually due to severe widespread brain damage. Patients with dementia form the largest segment of this group;

a few lose their social veneer as a consequence of a tumour situated at the front of the brain. It is at least comforting that patients are usually unaware of the distress and unpleasantness associated with their lack of bowel control. The suffering tends to be entirely on the side of onlookers and helpers. When incontinence takes the form of uncontrolled watery diarrhoea, which is lost almost continuously, it is essential that a search is made for severe constipation. This paradox is difficult for a layman to accept; however, when a patient with reduced powers of awareness becomes very constipated a large hard stool may be acting as a blockage to the bowel. Motions higher up may then liquefy, and ooze past the obstruction to run unhindered from the anus. Removal of the blockage (an unpleasant procedure for all concerned) and correction of the stool consistency help attempts to regain bowel control.

Patients who have persistent faecal incontinence and are aware of their problem are likely to have either a neurological condition affecting the spinal cord, such as severe trauma, a growth or a degenerative condition. Alternatively they may have a local destructive lesion affecting the normal opening and closing mechanisms of the lower end of the bowel. A growth or gross laxity of the muscles so that the bowel can prolapse or turn inside out are the most likely explanations. Both are easily detected by simple examination and can be corrected by surgical operation.

Transient faecal incontinence. Many transient episodes of incontinence are unfortunate accidents, with the patient literally being caught short. Even fit young people may have such embarrassing accidents if they suffer from an excessively explosive attack of diarrhoea. In older and frailer people the diarrhoea is equally troublesome even when not explosive, particularly when the patient's speed and mobility are hindered by painful arthritis or clumsiness due to a stroke. The awkward combination of loose motions, slow locomotion, and a distant toilet may be more than many disabled people can manage. In these cases attention to their walking and the location of their toilet is as important as consideration of possible causes for the loose motions.

If uncertainty about control remains after proper deliberation has been paid to all aspects of continence, then other methods of management must be contemplated. Special padded pants are available and can avoid

128

much embarrassment and unpleasantness, but they should only be used as a last measure of defence.

Colostomy or ileostomy. Another group of patients with limited control over bowel evacuation consist of those with a colostomy or ileostomy. These are patients who have had an operation to remove a portion of their large bowel, and this shortened bowel is brought to an artificial opening on the abdominal wall to replace the anus functionally. This is a mutilating operation and is only performed in serious circumstances where there is no reasonable alternative. Many patients are unduly apprehensive about the procedure fearing that they will smell and constantly become socially unacceptable. However, these worries are unjustified as the opening is covered with a sealed bag which can be easily cared for and emptied at convenient times. The patient can then continue to lead a normal and active life in every way.

Altered bowel habit

This symptom has already been mentioned above in the sections on diarrhoea and constipation. However, its importance justifies repetition. Any persistent alteration in a lifetime's bowel habit merits reporting to the doctor. The change can be the onset of constipation, persistent diarrhoea or alternation between constipation and looseness of the motions. Any of these symptoms may herald the presence of a serious underlying bowel problem. Early reporting and subsequent investigation will help to identify many problems at a time when curative treatment is still possible.

Although many benign conditions may present in this way, it is also a common and early form of presentation for cancer of the large bowel, and so for this reason must be taken seriously. If the change in bowel habit is also associated with the passage of blood, either fresh bright-red blood or dark altered blood, there is again the risk of an underlying malignant cause.

Diet

The essentials of a healthy diet have already been described in Chapter 3.

However special dietary problems and needs are likely to arise in times of ill-health. During a brief transient illness, the first essential is the maintenance of a good fluid intake, as the normal thirst mechanism seems to be reduced in the elderly further impairment is likely to occur during an illness. But so long as small and frequent drinks are taken the complications of dehydration can be avoided. The drinks should preferably contain some calorific value, the addition of glucose being the simplest method. In a more prolonged illness it is necessary to add further nutrients to such a liquid diet. Commercially prepared compounds such as Complan are freely available, and a mixture of milk, eggs and sugar also provide a nutritious liquid diet.

On these modified diets attention needs to be paid to the patient's bowels. When only fluids are taken there is the risk of constipation; and feeds thickened with dairy products and sugars can cause diarrhoea. The ill patient is likely to find the usually bulking foods unacceptable, and Celevac or Isogel may provide more readily consumed alternatives.

Specific illnesses require special diets and advice from a dietician is needed. Diabetics, for example must have a controlled amount of carbohydrate and limited fat intake. Patients with renal failure should have their protein intake restricted. In cases of pancreatic disease a low fat diet is desirable. In wasting malignant diseases, and chronic infections, extra protein supplements are beneficial. In all cases attractively presented food and the provision of favourite dishes is the most pleasant way of encouraging a flagging appetite.

15

Diseases of the heart, blood-vessels, and lungs

Atherosclerosis*

Arterial disease is the scourge of our time, certainly in the developed countries where it is in one form or another the predominant cause of death, as well as causing a great deal of suffering and disability. It is the underlying cause of most strokes, most heart attacks, and most leg amputations. In males, at least, it starts very early in life, during adolescence or even childhood. There is patchy thickening of the vessel wall by the deposition of cholesterol* and fibrous tissue, leading to partial obliteration of the interior of the artery. Finally, the flow through it may become so sluggish that the blood clots, or a microscopic leak of blood disrupts the arterial wall leading to sudden occlusion, or a clump of blood platelets detaches itself from a thickened plaque and lodges further down obstructing the blood flow to the area of tissue supplied. There are often two aspects to the process, therefore: gradual narrowing over a period of many years, which may or may not lead to overt ill-health, and the abrupt cessation of flow, which causes death (or infarction) of the area of tissue deriving its blood supply from the artery affected. Either way, the fundamental process is atherosclerosis*, and several factors are known to be involved in its development.

High blood pressure

A high blood pressure* carries an increased risk of both coronary heart disease and stroke. There is no doubt that successful control of the blood pressure by drug treatment, often lifelong, goes a long way towards restoring a normal life expectancy. The principal exception is the patient aged over 75, in whom it has yet to be convincingly demonstrated that reduction of a raised blood pressure confers much advantage.

Blood cholesterol*

The serum cholesterol is a major determinant of coronary risk. It is

131

linked, although not very closely, with the dietary consumption of saturated animal fat, and an increase in the proportion of polyunsaturated fats, mainly of plant origin, can retard the progress of atherosclerosis.

Cigarette smoking

This is the third major risk factor, and stopping smoking lengthens the odds against a cardiovascular catastrophe.

Less important factors

Among these may be mentioned: diet, lifestyle, diabetes and heredity.

Diet. Other ingredients may play a part, in addition to the quantity and type of fat, and it is clear that the majority of our energy intake should come from carbohydrate rather than fat sources. It is interesting to note that the diet of the civilian population of the United Kingdom during the Second World War was healthier, in the light of modern knowledge, than is our present diet (Fig. 10). Dietary fibre is thought to be helpful and to exert a protective influence. An excessive calory intake, resulting in obesity, almost certainly encourages the development of arterial disease. A high salt intake is thought to predispose to hypertension.

Life-style. Exercise appears to be beneficial and to offer a degree of protection against cardiovascular catastrophes (see Chapter 8). Though difficult to prove, many people believe that stress predisposes to coronary heart disease. There is indeed some evidence that those individuals who habitually exhibit what is known as type A behaviour (driving, striving, ambitious, aggressive) are at a greater risk than their more placid and easygoing contemporaries (type Bs). It also appears to be better to live in a hard water area.

Diabetes. One of the complications of diabetes* is the development of widespread arterial disease, and gangrene of the toes is a distressing example. The vessels involved are often the smaller branches of the arterial tree, so that the result may be less devastating than in the non-diabetic variety of gangrene.

Heredity. Most authorities are agreed that it pays to choose one's parents wisely! It is probable that heredity does play a part in atherosclerosis, but it is difficult to separate its effects from the environmental influences affecting the family, such as similarity of diet, of climate, and of habits.

Protein	12%	Protein	12%	Protein	12%
Fat	42%	Fat	30%	Fat	34%
Carbohydrate	46%	Carbohydrate	58%	Carbohydrate	53%
Today		Recommended		Second World War	

Fig. 10. The percentage energy derived from carbohydrate, protein, and fat.
Sources: *National food survey*, Household Food Consumption in the second quarter of 1982. HMSO, London; *Urban working class household diet 1940–1949* First Report of the National Food Survey, Ministry of Food. HMSO, London; Select Committee on Nutrition and Human Needs US Senate; *Dietary goals for the US* Government Printing Office, New York (1977).

The effects of arterial disease

Atherosclerosis affects the coronary arteries,* causing coronary heart disease or ischaemic heart disease, as it is sometimes known (ischaemia* means inadequacy of the blood supply). This is easily the commonest form of heart disease in this country, followed by the effects of hypertension which, as we have seen, leads to atherosclerosis and is thus very similar. It affects the arteries to the brain, causing stroke, although once again some strokes are the direct effect of high blood pressure. Most are the result of progressive narrowing of the carotid arteries and their branches consequent upon some or all of the factors mentioned above. It affects the arterial supply to the limbs and, rarely, to the intestine, kidneys, spinal cord, and other structures.

133

Coronary heart disease

There are four main ways in which the heart can be affected by diseased coronary arteries.

Angina pectoris

This is the symptom produced when the coronary vessels provide an adequate blood supply to the heart muscle at rest, but are too narrow to carry the augmented supply required to meet the increased oxygen demands of exercise. The heart muscle protests when called upon to perform extra work without extra pay, and the patient experiences the characteristic tight, aching pain in the centre of the chest, perhaps radiating across the chest to the shoulders and arms, occurring when walking (especially hurrying) and generally settling down within a few minutes of stopping. Many patients live for many years with their symptoms unchanged, although a few sustain heart attacks — and some thereafter paradoxically feel much fitter. A few develop their symptoms after increasingly trivial exertion or even at rest; this is a danger signal and may also become extremely incapacitating.

Treatment. The usual treatment is initially to check the general health, and this includes advice about smoking and obesity and perhaps the treatment of hypertension. The patient is given a supply of glyceryl trinitrate tablets which should be placed under the tongue to dissolve and not chewed or swallowed. This drug causes the vessels to expand, resulting in a headache and relief of the angina. It is much more effective if taken before the pain and can then prevent the attack. Many patients know perfectly well from experience which activities are likely to provoke an attack: it may be the seventh hole with the rather steep climb, or it may be sexual intercourse or the walk to the bus stop. Glyceryl trinitrate is a safe, effective, and long-established remedy, and is now available in the form of a spray which may possibly be more rapid in its effect. The tablets only last for eight weeks in storage, and even less if kept in a clear bottle or in a warm place, but the spray lasts much longer. For those whose symptoms are more severe, a similar preparation (isosorbide) is available for regular (for example, thrice daily) use or glyceryl trinitrate paste can be applied to the skin and will then be effective for six to 24 hours. Another group of pharmaceuticals, the beta-blocking drugs, may dramatically improve life though inevitably at the expense of certain adverse effects. There is yet a third group of drugs called calcium antagonists which can be used in conjunction with vasodilators (a drug that dilates small blood vessels and lowers blood pressure) or beta-blockers.

Heart attacks (coronary thrombosis, myocardial infarction*)

The term myocardial infarction indicates death of a part of the heart muscle, and this occurs when the coronary artery or its branch becomes obliterated or almost obliterated so that the affected part of the muscle becomes effectively starved of blood. The predominant symptom is classically the rapid onset of chest pain, qualitatively similar to angina but quantitatively much greater in severity and duration. The patient is often shocked, and is restless, pale, cold and sweaty. Vomiting and breathlessness may add to the patient's distress.

As is well known, this is a very serious disease with a high mortality, particularly within the first few hours, and some subjects drop dead virtually instantaneously. The death rate within the first six weeks is somewhere around 25 per cent, and about half these deaths occur within the first two hours — from complications such as shock, acute heart failure, and particularly cessation of an effective circulation because electrical overexcitability of the heart muscle makes the ventricles quiver uselessly instead of beating rhythmically. With each succeeding day, the infarct heals progressively to form a firm scar, and there is no reason at all why full activity should not be resumed within three months of the original attack. This can include gardening, tennis, sex, everything except smoking.

Treatment. There is general agreement concerning the treatment of the more disastrous complications, but very little about the logistical aspects of making emergency care available during those critical early hours. Ideally, lay people should be familiar with the recognition of circulatory arrest (no pulse can be detected in any of the great arteries by those who know where to feel) and the basic techniques of resuscitation, principally external cardiac massage and mouth-to-mouth ventilation. Some localities have experimented with cardiac ambulances staffed by specially trained doctors or ambulance men, but there is little evidence that such a service can be delivered on a large-scale and cost-effective basis. The same appears to be true of coronary care units in hospital, although they are undoubtedly capable of saving life in the severe and complicated case. For the less gravely ill patient, there seems to be a good case for believing that care at home, with frequent visits from the family doctor, is just as good, provided that the home circumstances permit. And when there are no serious complications, it only seems to be necessary to spend a few days in bed, when it is vitally important to keep the leg muscles working to prevent leg vein thrombosis.

Heart attacks, particularly in advanced age, can take a number of untypical forms. The patient may develop heart failure, or irregularity of the heart beat, or may have a fall or a blackout or a queer, dizzy turn, or may just feel rather off-colour, perhaps with some mild discomfort which is dismissed as being a form of indigestion. Establishing the diagnosis may not be of critical importance, since no one over the age of 70 should be encouraged to take to their beds for even a few days, unless they feel too ill to be up and about.

Heart failure

Heart failure is the final common path of every type of heart trouble, coronary artery disease being far and away the commonest cause in the western world. As the pumping action of the heart becomes feebler, it becomes unable to cope with all the blood being returned to it by the great veins, and a back pressure builds up. If this happens acutely, this affects primarily the lungs, which become waterlogged with fluid filling the air spaces (pulmonary oedema) so that there is rapidly progressive breathlessness. This medical emergency often comes on during the night. The sufferer may have noticed some difficulty with the breathing before, particularly if lying flat in the bed, and may have been in the habit of sleeping well propped up with pillows. On this occasion, he is too short of breath to be capable of sustained speech, and sits up on the edge of the bed, perhaps with an alarming bubbliness of the respiration. The family doctor can often bring about rapid relief by the intravenous injection of a diuretic* which will disperse the fluid and cause it to be eliminated as urine. Morphine is another traditional and extremely effective remedy, and oxygen will probably be administered in the ambulance as most of these patients need to be admitted to hospital for further treatment.

Diseases of the heart, blood-vessels, and lungs

Congestive cardiac failure. Heart failure which develops more gradually is known as congestive cardiac failure because it also leads to the accumulation of fluid, but of rather more widespread distribution. There is congestion of the lungs, but it is less dramatic in onset with increasing shortness of breath on increasingly trivial exertion such as mounting the stairs, walking, or even dressing and undressing. The legs fill with fluid and can be indented by means of digital pressure; this is known as oedema, and need not necessarily indicate heart disease but may occur in a variety of conditions including simply sitting about all day with the legs dependent — a long flight, for example, can have this effect on the healthiest of us. The sheet anchor of the treatment of congestive failure is again diuretic drugs, but this time they can be taken in tablet form; they may well be required on a long-term basis, although it must never be assumed that they will be required for life, and it is always worth trying the effect of stopping them after a few weeks — under medical supervision.

There is a large variety of diuretics for the doctor to choose from, and some, such as bendrofluazide, are very gentle, but others, such as frusemide, are much stronger, and may cause an inconveniently copious flow of urine for a few hours after taking them. They are all capable of a wide range of adverse effects, including salt and water loss or dehydration, causing weakness, dizziness, and perhaps thirst; incontinence or retention of urine; loss of potassium, again causing weakness; an attack of gout in those liable to it; and precipitating diabetes or disturbing its control. It is usual to give simultaneous potassium supplements, generally large tablets to be dissolved in water, which adds to the burden of medication.

Disorders of the heartbeat

Like heart failure, disorders of the heartbeat may occur in almost every variety of heart disease, and although frequently indicative of coronary artery disease, in old people the problem is often a simple fibrosis of the electrical conducting tissues of the heart. A degree of cardiac irregularity due to extra beats (or dropped beats when they are too weak to be felt at the wrist) is very common at all ages but especially in the elderly and is generally of little significance. Because the normal regular beat at 50-90 per minute is the most efficient rate and rhythm, any

137

marked departure may itself precipitate heart failure. Transient abnormalities may cause palpitations, and occasionally may cause a drop in the blood flow to the brain resulting in faints or falls. The diagnosis may require an electrocardiogram recorded for 24 hours by a portable tape recorder. The number of disturbances of the heart rhythm is enormous, but two are particularly worthy of mention.

Atrial fibrillation. This is the commonest abnormal rhythm, and may be found in perhaps 10 per cent of apparently healthy subjects over 65. The pulse is totally irregular, and although initially this may happen intermittently, the rhythm eventually becomes permanent. The effect depends entirely on the rate, which may be impossible to determine by counting the wrist pulse because some of the beats are too feeble to be felt, so that it will be necessary to count the heart sounds using a stethoscope. If the true rate of the ventricle is over 100, the doctor will probably wish to reduce it by administering digoxin (Lanoxin) tablets so that the ventricles have time to fill properly and can thus maintain their output.

Heart block. Heart block, like most of these disorders, is commonest in the old. The conduction of the electrical impulse transmitting the heartbeat from one part of the heart to another is interrupted, leaving the ventricles to 'do their own thing'. Like many of us, they are inclined to become idle when released from the pressure of higher authority, and in the simplest form of heart block they beat away regularly at the leisurely pace of 30 or 40 beats a minute. Although they have plenty of time to permit adequate filling, the output of the heart may fall simply due to the slowness of the rate, with restriction of the patient's exercise tolerance — the amount of activity he or she can undertake without distress.

Even more seriously, some of these patients are liable to episodes of effective circulatory arrest when the ventricles take an unauthorized break, and this produces abrupt loss of consciousness with the patient falling to the ground if standing at the time. These so-called Stokes-Adams attacks need to terminate with a spontaneous resumption of cardiac activity within three minutes if brain damage or death is to be avoided, and some do and some do not. The initial treament is to regard each attack as sudden death and to institute emergency measures, starting with a blow to the chest followed by heart massage if this does not do the trick. Anyone who recovers from one of these attacks is at grave risk, and is an urgent candidate for the insertion of an artificial pacemaker to regulate the heart's action.

Other cardiovascular disease

High blood pressure

Many references will be found throughout this book to the hazards of a high blood pressure, and the susceptibility of hypertensive subjects to arterial disease, stroke, and coronary heart disease. This is especially true in the young and middle-aged, in whom there is no doubt that treatment is beneficial. It remains true in the early 70s, but the benefits of treatment are much less clearcut at this age and large-scale studies are in progress which should provide a definitive answer within the next few years. Meanwhile, it remains clear that many older people feel less well on their medication, and that it may even be hazardous, and may for example lower the blood pressure too effectively. The drugs which are used include the diuretics, the beta-blockers, the vasodilators, the calcium antagonists, and methyldopa. There is an unnecessarily large array of preparations on the market, many of them containing mixtures of different drugs in one tablet, and if the doctor does feel that treatment is advisable, he should start with a small dose of one of the gentler drugs. The object is to avoid the complications of hypertension, and not because there is any likelihood of symptoms due to the blood pressure itself. For those who like precise definitions, over the age of 60 a blood pressure level over 175/100 (mmHg) is regarded as constituting hypertension.

Low blood pressure

A low blood pressure, on the other hand, may well cause symptoms in the elderly, and if the blood supply to the brain falls sharply, feelings of dizziness or faintness or actual loss of consciousness may occur. A fall in blood pressure is particularly likely to occur on standing up, for instance when getting out of a warm bed at night or in the morning or when getting out of the bath. Sometimes this is because the nervous pathways which normally prevent such occurrences have stopped functioning. Sometimes it is caused by the drugs used to treat hypertension or by certain drugs used for other purposes, and sometimes it is due to dehydration or myocardial infarction. If no remediable cause can be found, there are several drug treatments which are worth trying. The condition is much commoner than is generally realized and may have serious consequences.

Disease of the leg arteries

The great artery supplying the leg sometimes becomes blocked suddenly and the leg becomes cold, painful, and blue and white and blotchy. Urgent hospital treatment is required to try to save the leg. More often, the process is a gradual one, due to progressive atherosclerotic obliteration rather than to clotting of the blood. When the vessel is too narrow to allow the increased blood flow needed when the muscles are working, the characteristic symptom is a cramp-like pain in the calf on walking a certain distance, which passes off on stopping. This symptom is analogous to angina, and is called *intermittent claudication*. As is the case with angina, provided the patient stops smoking the condition often remains stable or gradually improves over a period of many years, particularly if the patient is encouraged to take exercise and repeatedly walk up to, and through the onset of pain.

In a few patients, the narrowing continues inexorably, and the walking distance progressively diminishes until eventually the artery is unable to supply sufficient blood for the needs of the limb at rest. The pain which occurs at rest is usually felt in the foot, may be very severe, and is often worst at night. In some cases, particuarly in very old and frail people who are not really mobile, rest pain is the first indication of the disease. It is not only a very distressing situation, but also a serious one, because it is likely to progress to ulceration and finally to gangrene of the extremity. The best hope is surgery or, more recently, the passage of a tube down the artery with a balloon which is then inflated to widen the narrowed segment and increase blood flow. If this is not feasible, and life is to be preserved, since gangrene is a life-threatening condition, amputation will be necessary. This is generally performed above the knee, although a much more limited operation may be possible in diabetics in whom it is often the very small vessels which are affected.

140

Diseases of the heart, blood-vessels, and lungs

Will the patient ever walk with his artificial leg? The response to re-habilitation depends much more on determination and on biological age rather than chronological age. It depends on being mentally well preserved, it depends on the state of the other arteries, especially those of the other leg, and it depends on the state of the hip joints and the heart and the lungs. There are about 65 000 amputees in the United Kingdom, most of them well over 60, because the operation is much more often performed for arterial disease than for trauma. Of these 10 per cent come to double amputation, and will require a wheelchair, but even then, given courage and a pair of strong arms, an independent life is entirely possible.

Thrombosis of the leg veins: blood clots in the lungs

When the blood clots in one of the deep veins of the thigh or calf, the leg typically becomes swollen, painful, tender, and a little bluish. This occasionally occurs after a surgical operation, but can also happen spontaneously and for no apparent reason. And occasionally a part of the clot detaches itself, travels up the great veins of the trunk and through the heart to enter the pulmonary arteries which carry blood from the heart to the lungs to be oxygenated. This is known as a pulmonary embolus,* and it will obstruct a branch of the pulmonary artery to cause damage, or infarction,* of the segment of lung tissue supplied, with fever, cough perhaps productive of some blood, chest pain, breathlessness, faintness, or other symptoms. If the clot is a massive one, it may even obstruct the output of the heart and can be rapidly fatal. Unfortunately, an embolus can occur without any warning signs in the legs. Pulmonary embolus is always treated with anticoagulants for several weeks or months, and deep vein thrombosis is usually treated similarly, but for a shorter period. These drugs prevent the blood from clotting and are therefore potentially dangerous and require adjustment of the dose by regular blood checks. It is necessary to issue the patient with a card indicating that he or she is receiving this treatment, and that any change in other medication can easily disturb the control. This includes aspirin and also alcohol.

Other lung diseases

Pneumonia

Pneumonia is an infection of the lungs which can be caused by a wide variety of bacteria and viruses and intermediate organisms. It can be localized to one part of one lung (lobar pneumonia) or it can be scattered in a patchy fashion throughout both lungs (bronchopneumonia). Either type is of common occurrence in the old, and is especially likely to attack those who are frail and debilitated, so that it is a common complication of heart failure, influenza, bronchitis, cancer, and stroke. Because it usually causes little suffering, it is sometimes known as 'the old man's friend' and offers a merciful release from advanced illness. In fitter subjects it usually responds well to antibiotic treatment and physiotherapy. Cough, breathlessness, fever, weakness, and (though less commonly) chest pain are the usual symptoms. One particular variety of pneumonia which has attracted considerable attention since the first outbreak was described in 1976 is *legionnaires' disease*. Cases have occurred both in outbreaks and sporadically in the United States, United Kingdom, Spain and elsewhere and there is a predilection for the sick and for those with chronic respiratory disease. Fever, headache, confusion, drowsiness, prostration, and diarrhoea may precede breathlessness and cough by two or three days.

Bronchitis

Acute bronchitis is similar to pneumonia although less serious since the infection has only reached the airways and not the lung substance. It causes a cough with some scanty, yellowish phlegm.

Chronic bronchitis is a common, disabling, potentially serious condition directly caused by smoking cigarettes. The irritant effect of the smoke causes the secreting cells in the bronchial lining to multiply and to produce increased quantities of mucus, so that the cardinal feature is the expectoration of sputum on most days for at least three months of the year. Continued smoking results in progression of the disease, with an enhanced risk of the following complications:

(1) *Infective exacerbations*, when the sputum changes from clear, frothy mucus to thick, yellow or green pus. These in turn may develop into pneumonia, and because of the damage sustained by the lungs,

the exchange of oxygen and carbon dioxide between the blood and the atmosphere cannot take place efficiently. Accumulation of carbon dioxide and lack of oxygen is called respiratory failure, and is very grave.

(2) *Chronic inflammation of the airways* causes swelling of the lining of the walls, and narrowing of the air passages. This stage is chronic obstructive airway disease and leads to wheezing and respiratory distress. Physical training can improve exercise tolerance in this situation.

(3) *Progressive lung damage* leads to diminishing exercise tolerance and breathlessness on trivial exertion.

(4) An increasing *strain on the heart* culminates in heart failure.

Occupational lung disease (such as coalminer's pneumoconiosis) is clinically similar in its effects and nowadays is most often seen in retired workers since legislation has provided more effective protection of the workforce.

Asthma

Most of us regard asthma as a disease of children and young people, but it can develop over the age of 60 even in subjects with previously healthy lungs. Spasm of the muscle in the bronchial walls causes constriction of the airways with the resulting tight, wheezing difficulty with breathing out and cough, the attacks often taking place at night. It is the extreme variation which distinguishes the airway obstruction of asthma from that of chronic bronchitis, and this distinction is a most important one because it often responds very favourably to treatment. There are numerous drugs available to relax the muscle and dilate the bronchi, and during an attack they are best taken by means of a pressurized aerosol inhaler so long as the inhalation technique is correct. It may be necessary to take regular medication in tablet form, and in more severe cases this might consist of corticosteroid preparations on a long-term basis. It is important to be familiar with some of the effect of these drugs, for example the dangers of running out or failing to adhere to the prescribed dosage. A card is carried indicating the type and dose of steroid. Really severe attacks are dangerous, and these may be recognized by severe wheezing, inability to speak whole sentences without pausing for breath, and a pulse rate of 120 per minute; medical attention is required under these circumstances.

Tuberculosis

This has now become a disease of immigrants and of the elderly only in the United Kingdom. Old men living alone in conditions of self-neglect and malnutrition are particularly susceptible, especially if the alcohol intake is higher than it should be. Patients on steroids are also at risk of flaring up their old, healed, unrecognized tuberculous foci. Once detected, it can usually be satisfactorily treated.

Cancer of the lung

This common and justifiably dreaded disease is directly related to cigarette smoking, and the risk recedes quite steeply when the habit is given up. By the time the diagnosis is made, the growth has usually spread too extensively for surgical excision to offer any great hope of a cure, but the degree of malignancy varies considerably, and sometimes it takes a very slow course over many months or years. Pain from the primary tumour or from distant deposits, for instance in the bones, usually responds very well to radiotherapy.

Choking

This is mentioned because it is an avoidable cause of death and because it is fairly common, since over 3000 Americans choke to death each year. It is commonest in infancy, but among adults then increases in frequency again in late middle and old age, in common with pneumonia. A partially masticated lump of food is inhaled and lodges in the larynx with very little warning, and this seems to happen more readily if the subject has taken an appreciable quantity of alcohol. The victim may raise his hand to his throat, and even if unable to answer, may nod if directly asked if he is choking. He is unable to speak or breathe, rapidly becomes pale and then blue, and loses consciousness and collapses. The onlooker may be deceived into suspecting a massive heart attack ('the café coronary') but cardiac resuscitation is unhelpful. In public places, embarrassment may lead the victim into the exceedingly unwise reaction of getting up unnoticed and making his exit into the lavatory, where he may die within seconds. The correct treatment is Heimlich's manoeuvre, in which a sudden upwards thrust by the clapsed fists around the upper abdomen from behind, repeated as necessary, forces the diaphragm up, expelling air and, hopefully, the food mass, from the upper airway.

Sleep apnoea

A serious problem which is attracting increasing medical attention is that of obstruction of the upper airway occurring intermittently during the night, especially in the obese and those with chronic bronchitis or enlarged tonsils and adenoids. It is commoner in men than women. It causes temporary cessation of respiration, or sleep apnoea. The pauses are ended by loud inspiratory snores, often followed by awakening.

There is a second variety of sleep apnoea, when the centres in the brain stem* which are responsible for maintaining the respiratory drive fail. This again leads to pauses in the breathing, and the condition is accentuated by alcohol or sedative drugs. These disorders are probably commoner in later life than is generally realized. The results include sudden death during the night, morning headache, daytime drowsiness, personality changes, and adverse effects on the heart. The usual age of onset is 45–50 and severity may increase with age.

16

Feeling off-colour

There is a widespread conspiracy to deprive older people of proper medical attention. This is especially prevalent where the complaint is a rather undramatic one, perhaps just a vague feeling of 'going off a bit' or being rather off-colour or out of sorts for a few weeks or a month or two. Very often, when these feelings are confided to the family, the response is 'Well what can you expect at your age?' Even when medical advice is sought, it is regrettably not unknown for a swift consultation to be terminated with the reassuring words 'Well what can you expect at your age?' Eventually, the patient himself or herself becomes a party to the conspiracy and accepts, with a sigh of resignation, 'I expect it's just my age' — perhaps relieved at the excuse not to admit to the fear that he or she may have fallen prey to some terrible disease.

This possibility is undeniable, but it is one of the messages of this book that never (which, in medicine, means hardly ever) should symptoms be ascribed simply to age and ignored on that account. It is entirely possible to feel perfectly well in one's late 80s and the authors have encountered many people who vehemently claim to do so. It is worth emphasizing that medicine has a great deal to offer to the aged, despite their own feelings that there may not be much that the doctor can do for them and that they may be wasting his time. Some diseases respond very satisfactorily to treatment, even if they cannot necessarily be cured in the strict sense of the term. Most others can be ameliorated and life thereby made much more comfortable and worthwhile. It is usually possible to minimize the disability caused by the illness and thus enable the patient to remain active and independent. Much can be done for the old, and they should not be encouraged to endure their symptoms stoically in the belief that they are an inseparable accompaniment of the passing years.

Everyone knows that something needs to be done if one falls down unconscious and has a fit, or vomits up blood, or has a stroke. But now let us pretend, instead, that the reader is Mrs X, aged perhaps in the early 70s, and that one or more of the following things start to go wrong over a period of a few weeks or a month or two:

You have no energy, you feel overcome by lassitude, lethargy, fatigue. You feel physically weak and weary and everything is too much effort. You notice widespread, vague, ill-defined aches and pains and discomfort, none of which add up to a single clear-cut pain. You are off both food and fluids and you are losing weight.

Now try to imagine, instead, that you are Mrs X's daughter, for, despite what has been said, most families are genuinely concerned and anxious to obtain the best possible care and advice for their ageing members, and indeed it is often on the initiative of a relative that medical help is sought at all. Although she says very little about her health, you are becoming increasingly worried about mother because you have noticed one or more of the following changes over the past few weeks or a month or two.

She seems to be so much less active and does less and less about the place. She is becoming less mobile and is effectively housebound, possibly even room- or chair-bound. She may have had the odd fall; she has lost all her 'go' and sparkle, and always seems tired and withdrawn. She is becoming unable to look after herself. She is not eating or drinking and is obviously losing weight.

Causes of 'going off'

The possible causes of such a state of affairs are legion, and the following is an incomplete list:

Anaemia
Cancer
Constipation (see Chapter 14)
Dementia (see Chapter 10)
Depression (see Chapter 10)
Diabetes
Drugs (including alcohol) (see Chapter 17)
Fluid and electrolyte balance disturbed

Giant cell arteritis
Heart disease (see Chapter 15)
Kidney failure
Parkinson's disease (see Chapter 11)
Polycythaemia (too many red cells in the blood)
Stomach ulcer (see Chapter 14)
Subdural haematoma (blood clot under the skull)
Thyroid disorders
Tuberculosis and other chronic infections
Vitamin deficiency

Anaemia

Anaemia* is a reduction in the concencentration of haemoglobin, the oxygen-carrying pigment in the blood. The haemoglobin is contained in the red blood cells, and these are produced in the red bone marrow and survive for 100–120 days in the circulation before undergoing destruction and being replaced by new ones. Anaemia can be caused through several different mechanisms.

Deficiency of essential nutrients

Iron. Iron is a constituent of haemoglobin, and iron deficiency results in an anaemia in which the cells are small and contain less haemoglobin. This sometimes arises due to an inadequate dietary intake, the chief sources being meat, egg yolk, green vegetables, and fruit. But the commonest form of anaemia is iron deficiency due to chronic blood loss, and apart from menstruation this is most likely to occur from the gut. Oesophagitis due to hiatus hernia, peptic ulcer, cancer of the stomach, and cancer of the large bowel (see Chatper 14) may all declare themselves in this way. Blood may ooze gently from the stomach in people taking certain drugs and aspirin and other drugs used for arthritis are particularly liable to have this effect. Sometimes the bleeding is brisk, but this is an unmistakable emergency and will result in vomiting blood or passing black stools and becoming shocked.

Vitamin B$_{12}$ (cyanocobalamin). This is required for the production of red cells. Deficiency is most commonly seen in pernicious anaemia, in

148

which the stomach lining fails to produce a substance which is essential to enable the B_{12} to be absorbed from the intestine. The red cells are large in this condition. The brain, spinal cord and peripheral nerves can also be affected by B_{12} deficiency.

Folic acid. This plays a similar role to vitamin B_{12} and lack of it leads to a similar type of anaemia. This may occur through dietary deficiency, particularly in alcoholics, green vegetables, meat and cereals being the main sources. Certain intestinal disorders and drugs are rarely responsible for folic acid or B_{12} deficiency.

Bone marrow and disease

The bone marrow may be directly affected and may for example be invaded by cancer or fibrous tissue, or it may be adversely affected by generalized disease such as tuberculosis, cancer, kidney failure, under-activity of the thyroid*, and many others. It can also be poisoned by certain drugs, and may then cease to manufacture red cells and/or white cells to combat infection and/or platelets to enable the blood to clot, both of which are extremely serious situations.

As well as the rather non-specific weakness and loss of energy depicted above, anaemia can cause dizziness, breathlessness, and heart failure, but surprisingly often it seems to cause very little disturbance to the health especially if it develops gradually. Its main importance, it will be appreciated, is that it may be a sign of serious and deep-seated disease, so that it is incumbent on the doctor to determine the cause of the anaemia. The appearance of the blood sample under the microscope will give a good idea; iron, B_{12}, and folic acid can be measured in the blood to confirm the diagnosis, but if the appearance suggests iron deficiency it may be necessary to test the stool chemically for blood and arrange X-ray examinations of the gut to look for a cause.

A severe degree of anaemia due to marrow involvement or iron deficiency may require transfusion, but the more usual treatment is simple replacement of iron in tablet form, folic acid in tablet form, or B_{12} by injection every month or so — together with treatment of the underlying disease, if any.

Cancer

A cancer is a malignant growth which arises due to the uncontrolled multiplication of abnormal primitive cells usually starting in a single focus although in a few varieties the affected tissue proliferates simultaneously in many different sites. Four stages can be broadly distinguished:

(1) *Local proliferation* results in a lump, swelling, or tumour. There may be a few symptoms or there may be serious results, depending on the situation (difficulty in swallowing if in the gullet, obstruction of the intestine, epilepsy and headache in the case of the brain).

(2) *Invasion and infiltration* causing ulceration of the skin or severe pain due to pressure on nerves.

(3) *Necrosis (death of tissue)* at the centre due to growth outstripping blood supply. This releases toxic substances and may cause loss of appetite, nausea, weight loss, and general ill-health.

(4) *Distant spread via the bloodstream* so that seedlings ('metastases') grow in bones, causing pain or fractures, the lungs, causing breathlessness, the liver, causing loss of appetite, and other remote sites.

Main types of cancer

The common cancers in the United Kingdom are as follows:

Lung (mainly men but increasing in women)
Breast (women)
Skin
Prostate in males
Cervix (neck) of uterus in females
Large bowel
Stomach
Rectum
Bladder (mainly men)

These are diseases of late life with the possible exception of cancer of the breast, but even this now has a peak incidence of 60 and a mortality rate increasing thereafter. It is also true that the degree of malignancy of some of these growths is extremely variable and that sometimes a cancer of the breast or prostate is only very slowly progressive.

Feeling off-colour

Tumours of the skin, breast and rectum are likely to become apparent through their local effects, but those of lung, stomach, and kidney may easily just give rise to the vague ill-health which we have been describing. Apart from the distant effects through blood-borne spread to other sites, they sometimes cause curious metabolic disturbances by producing biologically active substances.

Causes of cancer

Perhaps even more than most other diseases, prevention is a more promising objective than cure, and the key to prevention is knowledge of the causes. This knowledge has expanded considerably during the past 20 years, and some of the factors which have been implicated are as follows:

Tobacco — lung
Industrial exposure (e.g. asbestos) — lung
Industrial exposure (e.g. dyes) — bladder
Irradiation — leukaemias
Ultraviolet light — skin
Sexual promiscuity — neck of womb
Racial or environmental — stomach (Japan)
Virus — Burkitt's lymphoma, neck of womb
Other diseases — Paget's disease of bone, ulcerative colitis, cirrhosis, pernicious anaemia
Low fibre diet — bowel
Breast-feeding (by contrast) may afford some protection

Diabetes

Diabetes*, the presence of too high a level of glucose in the blood, is often thought of as a lifelong disorder rather than one which emerges with advancing years. In fact, if strict criteria are adhered to, the prevalence of the disease rises steadily with age, the peak age of onset being 67, but by no means all diabetics detected by blood tests have any symptoms or require treatment. Those elderly diabetics who have had the illness many years will probably need to continue with their insulin or other treatment. Those who develop it in their 60s, 70s, or

151

80s occasionally need insulin but more often the so-called 'maturity-onset' variety is less severe and less liable to the dangerous complication of diabetic coma. The onset may be quite symptomless or there may be a vague deterioration in the general health: sometimes there is thirst, weight loss and a tendency to pass large quantities of urine; and sometimes there may be a susceptibility to infection, particularly of the bladder, and itching around the private parts.

Treatment

If there are symptoms, treatment will probably be required, and the first step is the dietary correction of significant obesity. In those who are not particularly overweight, or whose symptoms persist following reduction, it is usual to prescribe a controlled diet in which, these days, most of the energy requirement is supplied in the form of carbohydrate rather than fat. The carbohydrate should be of the high-fibre unrefined polysaccharide type to be found in wholemeal bread and biscuits, wholegrain breakfast cereals (porridge, Weetabix, Shredded Wheat), all vegetables (especially pulses and potatoes in their jackets), all fruit, and brown rice. Monosaccharides (glucose) and disaccharides (sucrose) should be avoided, which precludes syrup, honey, jam, marmalade, chocolate (including the 'diabetic' variety which is both high in calories and expensive), sweets, cakes, pastries, ordinary biscuits, sweet drinks, tinned fruits, and sweetened cereals. This dietary control provides a basis for achieving a reasonably stable blood sugar in a substantial number. Other diabetics require tablets which stimulate the secretion of insulin by the pancreas (sulphonylureas), and a few need a different type of oral drug as well or instead (biguanides).

Urine testing

Although patients are usually advised to test the urine regularly in order to check the control of their diabetes, the amount of sugar in the urine is often a very inaccurate guide to the blood level, and a blood sugar measurement is advisable from time to time and is essential for those on insulin. Any acute illness is likely to disturb diabetic control, and so can diuretic drugs given to disperse accumulated fluid in other conditions such as heart failure. A simple device for obtaining a drop of blood from the finger is now available, and so is a small instrument to be kept at home for patients to undertake their own measurements.

Disturbances of fluid and electrolyte balance

It was emphasized in Chapter 9 that one of the fundamental frailties of the ageing organism is impairment of the ability to maintain a constant internal environment in terms of physics and chemistry in the face of challenges from the external environment.

Dehydration

Vomiting, diarrhoea, and diabetes are among the more obvious illnesses which may cause salt and water to be lost, but older people quite readily become dehydrated even without clearcut cause. One reason for this is the reduced capacity of the kidney to conserve salt and water by eliminating waste products in a small volume of highly concentrated urine. By the same token, there is some evidence that the old may not experience thirst as readily as the young, and some are reluctant to maintain an adequate fluid intake because of the fear of an urgent or frequent need to empty the bladder. The consequence is a low intake but a persistent output of moderate quantities of moderately dilute urine and a tendency to lose salt and water from the tissues leading to weakness, lassitude and perhaps a low blood pressure. Long-term medication with diuretics can produce identical results.

Loss of potassium

One particular electrolyte which may be lost from the body in the urine is potassium, and potassium depletion leads to muscular weakness and general loss of wellbeing. This again is especially likely to occur as a result of diuretic treatment, particularly as the diet may not contain an adequate intake. Meat and oranges are rich in potassium, but it is usual to give extra potassium in the form of tablets or medicine when diuretics are prescribed. Sometimes some extra potassium is incorporated in the diuretic tablet (which will then usually have a K added to the end of its name, K being the chemical symbol for potassium) and sometimes, instead, an additional drug is administered with the effect on the kidney of restricting the amount of potassium lost in the urine.

Giant cell arteritis

This mysterious disease is almost always confined to people over 55. It consists of an inflammatory process of unknown cause affecting the arteries of the scalp, tongue, jaw muscles, eye, and sometimes brain, so that severe headache and scalp tenderness are the most typical features. Fever, malaise, weight loss, and anaemia are common and may indeed dominate the clinical picture. Sometimes the illness starts off with generalized muscular aches and pains and stiffness, and this is called *polymyalgia rheumatica*. A simple blood test, or in more difficult cases removal of a segment of artery for microscopic examination, will establish the diagnosis, and treatment is then started with initially high doses of corticosteroids (prednisolone) which arrests the disease and prevents blocking of affected arteries which can otherwise cause blindness, stroke or heart attack. The response is dramatic with virtual disappearence of symptoms within 48 hours. The steroids are then gradually reduced to a maintenance dose which will probably need to be continued for at least two years.

Kidney failure

This may be a late result of long-term chronic low-grade renal infection, or it may be caused by back-pressure effects from an enlarged prostate leading to obstruction to the outflow of urine from the bladder, or it may be the end result of any of the rarer kidney diseases. The effects are anaemia and disturbance of the acid-base, water and electrolyte balance with rather non-specific feelings of illness. Water and electrolyte depletion will in turn adversely affect the kidneys, and so will a serious fall in blood pressure.

Polycythaemia

Polycythaemia is the opposite of anaemia, so that there is an excessively high level of haemoglobin in the blood and a rise in the proportion of whole blood which is formed by the cells. This proportion is usually between 35 and 50 per cent, but may be as high as 55 per cent in males without being necessarily indicative of disease. If the haemoglobin and the 'packed cell volume (pcv)*' are above normal, it may be due to polycythaemia, an uncommon disease of the bone marrow with certain analogies to leukaemia (in which too many white cells are produced). It is sometimes due to other diseases, and quite often to a reduction in the plasma volume rather than a true increase in the mass of red cells. The treatment will clearly be different — withdrawal of blood on the one hand, or rehydration on the other.

The importance of the subject lies partly in the dizziness and fatigue which may ensue, but mainly in the effect on the blood flow. Blood viscosity rises exponentially with the packed cell volume, and if the arteries are narrowed by disease the effect on the blood flow may be catastrophic. In these circumstances, even subjects with a 'high normal' haemoglobin occurring as a normal variant and not due to any disease process may benefit from the judicious removal of blood. Bloodletting is currently enjoying a new vogue in scientific medicine!

Subdural haematoma

A haematoma is a collection of blood which has accumulated within a tissue and outside the blood vessels where it belongs so that it forms a swelling like a large bruise. A subdural haematoma is situated between the skull and the brain which it is likely to damage by compression and is a not uncommon sequel of head injury in older people, although the injury may appear trivial at the time and indeed there is no history of trauma in 20 per cent of cases. The patient seeks medical advice within a period of two weeks to six months in chronic cases, and headache, personality changes, fits, one-sided limb weakness, and impairment of consciousness are common features. The diagnosis should be established by computerized tomography (CT), and a neurosurgeon will often be able to evacuate the blood through a hole drilled in the skull, although the mortality remains at about 45 per cent in patients over 60. This is partly because many are very old and frail, and partly because of diagnostic difficulties.

Thyroid disorders

An overactive thyroid in later years does not typically give rise to the

155

protuberant eyes, fleshy goitre, and hot, sweaty, irritable, jumpy demeanour which characterize the condition in the young. The effects are most marked on the heart, which may be rapid and irregular (atrial fibrillation, see Chapter 15), but weight loss, weakness and lassitude are also common. A blood test will usually give the diagnosis, and treatment is in the form of radioactive iodine given in a drink. In case this sounds too good to be true, it should be added that it will take some weeks to be effective, and that subsequent surveillance is necessary because the gland may become underactive in later years.

Hypothyroidism

Hypothyroidism (underactivity of the thyroid) is the disease *par excellence* whose features are shrugged off as being 'just old age'. There is a general slowing down, a sluggishness of thought, speech and action. There is impairment of memory and concentration, deafness, hoarseness, and constipation. The patient gains weight and becomes puffy and coarse of skin, complains of the cold, and the hair becomes thin. These changes take place so insidiously that those who see the patient regularly − the relatives, the family doctor − are usually quite oblivious to them. Treatment with thyroxine will revolutionize the patient's health and is extremely gratifying, but it must be given very cautiously so that it generally takes a couple of months to achieve the full benefit.

Tuberculosis and other chronic infections

Tuberculosis is mentioned in Chapter 15, but other infections are now increasingly seen in older subjects and may pursue a very silent and insidious course. Influenza and other virus illnesses often produce a general 'going off', but the course is more likely to be over a few days rather than weeks. An uncommon but important condition is bacterial endocarditis, formerly a dreaded complication of diseased heart valves following rheumatic fever but now sometimes encountered among people whose heart valves are affected by simple wear and tear and who are often quite unaware of any cardiac disability. Once again, anaemia, weight loss and malaise over a period of weeks may be the main effect of the disease, but without energetic antibacterial treatment the outlook is serious. Abscesses in the pelvis, liver or elsewhere are other infective conditions which may prove extremely reluctant to declare their hands.

Vitamin deficiency

One unworthy thought which deserves to be entertained by Mrs X's daughter is the possibility that her mother has increased her alcohol consumption to the detriment of her diet and of her general health. There are of course many other vitamin-deficient diseases, of which the most important in the present context and one of the most satisfactory to treat is osteomalacia (see Chapter 11).

Acute 'going off'

The same sort of picture may evolve much more dramatically and acutely, over hours or days rather than weeks or months. The features are likely to include profound weakness, taking to bed, failure to eat or drink, and perhaps some clouding of the consciousness. In persons of advanced years, the following possible causes should be considered:

Abdominal emergencies
Heart attack (see Chapter 15)
Hypothermia
Infections — influenza, pneumonia, septicaemia, urinary tract infections
Pulmonary thromboembolism (see Chapter 15)

Hypothermia

Accidental hypothermia is defined as a fall in the deep body temperature, as measured with a low-reading rectal thermometer, to 35 °C or below (95 °F). It is a condition which especially affects the old, the frail, the sick and the poor. It is caused by a combination of the following factors:

A cold environment
Defective homeostasis
Illness

A cold environment. Old peoples' homes may be cold because of poverty and poor housing, or because they have never adopted the central heating habit, or because they were taught to open the bedroom windows as children and have done so ever since, or because of the effort involved in lighting an open fire. Table 15 illustrates the findings of one survey of the living room temperatures of old people.

Table 15   *Living room temperatures*

Recommendation (minimum)	°C	°F	Percentage of sample below this temperature
By DHSS	21	70	90
By Parker Morris housing standards	18.3	65	75
By Offices, Shops & Railways Act	16	60.8	54
Well below comfort	12	53.6	10

Defective homeostasis. There is evidence that victims of hypothermia have impaired ability to detect environmental temperature differences, and tend not to respond to a fall in temperature as others would (wrapping up, closing windows, lighting a fire). There is also evidence that their physiological responses are impaired, and these comprise increasing heat production by shivering and reducing heat loss from the skin by closing down blood flow through the skin.

Illness. The precipitating factor may be a severe general illness such as pneumonia, or a fall from which the patient has been unable to recover, perhaps due to a fracture or stroke. Certain drugs, notably the major tranquillisers, render people more prone to hypothermia.

Features of hypothermia. Suspicion should be aroused by a cold house or room, and an ill old person whose abdomen feels cool to touch, particularly if she has been lying on the floor. Below a core temperature of 32 °C (90 °F), some clouding of conciousness is the rule, and muscular rigidity and a slow pulse are common. These patients are seriously ill and the mortality is high (below 30 °C (86 °F), about two out of three).

Treatment of hypothermia. Wrapping in a blanket and warming the room are the only first aid measures which can be recommended, and the temptation to administer hot drinks should be resisted. Hospital treatment is generally required.

Feeling off-colour

Prevention is preferable, and the house should be kept warm. Warm clothes are important, particularly a woolly nightcap, because almost half the body's heat loss is from the head, and low voltage electric overblankets are both safe and effective. A heating allowance may be obtainable from the Department of Health and Social Security (DHSS).

17

Medicines

There is a growing demand for drugs to prevent, retard, or ameliorate the adverse effects of ageing. About 30 per cent of all prescriptions are for those age 65 and over. Medical treatment, like diplomacy, is the art of the possible and modern medicines properly used have much to offer older folk. A careful appraisal of the nature of the illness or disability and of the overall condition of the patient is required so that the treatment given is wholly appropriate. Drugs are not the answer to all life's problems, and there is little doubt that a great deal of time and money is wasted on medicines; worse still, real detriment may actually be caused by drugs. Irrespective of age, some diseases are curable and some are not; age of itself has very little to do with it. Even when diseases are incurable a great deal can be done to help the person to live in reasonable comfort and to follow for as long as possible his normal way of life. For those more severely ill medicines can relieve some of the more distressing symptoms and ultimately secure a comfortable dignified death.

A breakdown in health of an elderly person may be due to an acute illness or to an acute episode in chronic illness already well established. Often multiple chronic diseases coexist and invite multiple drug treatments. Thus there is a risk that too many drugs will be prescribed simultaneously, and the elderly patient may be made worse by them.

Diagnosis for medical treatment

The key to good medical treatment is accurate diagnosis of all components of the patient's illness. The doctor then treats what is treatable in as safe and simple a manner as possible using the minimum number and dose of drugs necessary to achieve the desired effect. Diagnosis can be difficult because of the non-specific presentation of illness in aged people. Additionally the doctor may be persuaded to prescribe by the patient, his relatives, or other interested persons, when drugs have little or nothing to offer. Relatives striving to cope with a sick elderly person often insist that 'something must be done', with the danger that after a somewhat perfunctory examination of the problem the doctor might prescribe something in response to the clamour for action but without a well-reasoned scientific basis for the prescription. A large amount of prescribing is in response to social pressures and not surprisingly many prescriptions are useless and some are hazardous. An astonishing amount of prescribing for older patients appears to be unsatisfactory in this way. It is hoped that better training of doctors and others in the special needs of elderly people will do much to improve the management of illness in old age.

The burgeoning new pharmacology

During the last fifty years there has been a phenomenal growth in the pharmaceutical industry and as a result of much meticulous research many new and valuable drugs have been produced. Most of the drugs prescribed today did not exist even 25 years ago. Among the important newcomers are antibiotics, diuretics, antihypertensives, and drugs to alleviate the distressing symptoms of Parkinson's disease and to treat mental illness. The therapeutic value of some of these new drugs is so great it may give the impression that every illness should be treatable and even completely curable by drug use. Certainly a dramatic response to treatment may be seen in many illnesses, even in very elderly people.

Unfortunately the history of the pharmacological revolution is studded with sinister and occasionally catastrophic reminders of the harm that drugs can do. Examples are the phenothiazines, introduced in the 1950s, as tranquillizers were widely used to damp down restlessness and agitation in patients with mental illness. Although effective they were toxic when large doses were given for long periods and until these limitations were realized many cases of gross neurological disorder were produced; thalidomide was widely prescribed as a 'safe' hypnotic until the early 1960s when it was incriminated after long-term use as the cause of damage to the nervous system in adults and, with short-term use, of severe congenital malformations in some babies born of mothers who had taken the drug; practolol was used extensively to control heart rate and high blood pressure until it was reported in the 1970s to cause serious damage to the eyes and other parts of the body. The enormous benefits of the new pharmacology are not to be denied, but it is important for all concerned to realize that drugs which bring benefit can also cause harm and in any case there are strict limitations on what drugs can do especially in the general area of social malaise.

Excessive use of drugs by old people

Although modern medicines may be of great benefit to ill old people we are in danger of trivializing their use. A major problem is the unnecessary long-term use of drugs, especially those which affect the brain, heart, and blood-vessels. Very many patients can benefit by a reduction in chronic drug use (see below, p. 165). There seem to be two main reasons for overprescribing: firstly, many prescriptions are given for non-pharmacological reasons; and secondly, drugs are started without there being a specific mechanism for stopping them.

Drug abuse

A further reason for excessive long-term use of drugs is habituation,* often coupled with the belief that if the drug is stopped something terrible will happen to the workings of the body or the mind or both. Usually these fears are based on misconceptions which the patient needs to sort out with the doctor because in some cases the chronic use of the drug ultimately does harm. Common examples of drug abuse include:

(1) Long-term use of hypnotics and sedatives where the victim is 'hooked' on his drug, just as the alcoholic is 'hooked' on his drink, and where mental and nervous system deterioration may result. Stopping the drug may leave the person temporarily irritable, anxious and unable to sleep properly until the body readjusts to its normal (predrugged) state. Sadly, some people prefer to exist in a hazy world of sedation rather than face up to the realities of life with a clear mind.

(2) Long-term use of puratives by those obsessional people who flog their bowels mercilessly with medicines to the extent that normal colonic function is destroyed, and the body is depleted of potassium, and this can lead to profound weakness.

(3) Long-term use of diuretics which stimulate water excretion by the

162

kidney) in those cases where sitting still is the main cause of the swollen legs, and where the drug can cause incontinence, dehydration and salt depletion.

(4) Long-term use of pain relievers of the narcotic type. Addiction is well known to occur with morphine and heroin but milder opiates also cause a degree of dependence and they are commonly used in proprietary pain killers often accompanying paracetamol. The patient enjoys the psychic 'lift' of the opiate and misses this when the drug is withdrawn and so prefers to continue taking the tablets indefinitely.

Latent functions of the prescription

One of the reasons for overprescribing is that the prescription of a drug is not simply the provision of a pharmaceutical agent, which is likely to do good, but it is also symbolic of the physician's power to heal and it is a clearly visible example of the doctor at work. Instead of the doctor explaining to the patient that drug treatment is not necessary for a mild or transient illness a drug is often prescribed for this symbolic reason. It is, if you like, a symbol of science versus fate. The doctor (and often the patient too!) does not really believe that the prescription will alter the outcome in any specific pharmacological way.

Additionally, receipt of the prescription and the acquisition of the medicines is a validation of the sick status of the patient, and to a certain extent it represents patient achievement. The patient feels that he has actually gained something from the doctor or from the Health Service. The medicines are official recognition that the person is ill and cannot be expected to do all the things that non-sick people are expected to do. This gives some satisfaction, not just to the patient, but often also to his relatives and friends.

The prescription may be used by the doctor to 'buy' time while awaiting natural remission of the disease. The prescription may ward off the need for a proper medical explanation and possibly the admission by the doctor that orthodox medicine has nothing to offer the patient, and certainly it is not uncommonly used as a means of terminating the medical consultation. Thus many prescriptions are given for psychosocial rather than for pharmacological reasons.

Apparently doctors more than patients favour drug use as the

163

outcome of a medical consultation and many patients who go to the doctor for advice or reassurance are given a prescription instead. Family doctors who spend more time with their patients giving advice or reassurance tend to prescribe less. In one study, consultation times of five minutes per patient generated 20 per cent more prescriptions than ten-minute consultations.

Drug consumption in later life

Chronic repeat prescriptions become increasingly common with increasing age, as does the number of items prescribed for the patient (Fig. 11).

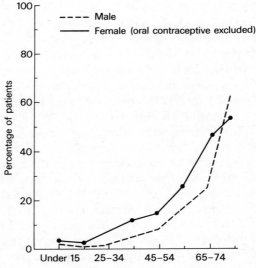

Fig. 11. Percentage of patients living at home prescribed medicines for 90 days or more. (After Murdoch 1980.)

It is estimated that some 70–80 per cent of people over the age of 75 years in Britain are on long-term repeat prescriptions and in addition 25–30 per cent of these also self-medicate. Two-thirds of regular drug users take one to three drugs each day while one-third of them take four to six drugs each day. Over a third of women in this age group are on long-term psychotropic* drugs and perhaps not surprisingly at least

164

Medicines

15 per cent of all admissions to geriatric wards are patients suffering from adverse reactions to drugs. Some 30 per cent of those on long-term drug treatment have little contact with their doctor and for a similar percentage the drugs are of little or no value, and for a similar percentage again (not necessarily the same people!) drugs are probably causing some unwanted effects. Because of the routine nature of repeat prescriptions and the large numbers involved, an increasing proportion of this work is transferred from the doctor to the hands of non-medically qualified prescription writers.

Adverse reactions and overconsumption. Adverse reactions to drugs are more common in the elderly than in the young, the incidence in the eighth decade being seven times that in the third. This is due to a bigger exposure to drugs and to less efficient drug elimination, especially by the kidneys. Impaired homeostasis is also a major factor. Side-effects which might be tolerable in the young could have disastrous effects on the old, especially if mental function or balance is disturbed. For these reasons smaller doses of drugs are usually required in old people.

Fortunately doctors are becoming increasingly aware of the problem of overprescribing and are devising ways to prevent it. Firstly, they are becoming reluctant to prescribe unless there is a valid scientific reason for the prescription, and secondly, they are instituting properly thought out prescribing policies backed by a medical records system designed to control the chronic use of drugs especially of sedatives and tranquillisers. Long-term repeats with infrequent medical review may be appropriate in patients with diabetes or rheumatoid arthritis, but more frequent review is often required in other cases, such as certain heart troubles or mental depression.

Compliance with the prescription. The prescription of a drug is just part of the story. The prescription must also be dispensed and the drugs taken by the patient in the way that the doctor ordered. When this aspect of medicine-taking has been explored it has been found that in elderly patients modest and occasionally serious deviation from doctor's orders occurred with more than half the prescribed medicines. If the patient knows what is wrong with him and what the doctor hopes to achieve by drug treatment, he will be more likely to co-operate. Clear written instructions are helpful and should be asked for if they are not offered.

When the medical advice given is simple, brief and specific, there is more chance that the old person will follow it (Table 16).

Table 16   *Advice to those taking medicines*

---

(1)   Obtain clear (preferably printed) instructions from the doctor or pharmacist.
(2)   Take the medicines regularly as prescribed, and report all unwanted effects.
(3)   Safeguard all medicines against:
       damp, heat, sunlight, accidental use by children, theft and subsequent abuse.
(4)   Discard unwanted drugs; consult the doctor or pharmacist about this.
(5)   Cooperate with the doctor to achieve minimum drug use compatible with your illness.

Minimizing the hazards

To avoid unnecessary hazards of drug treatment, while securing the benefits, we must be keenly aware of the many problems which drugs can produce and reduce drug use to a practicable minimum. Regular review of treatment will allow consideration for the reduction or discontinuation of each and every drug as soon as possible. Often the treatment which is given at the outset of an illness should be modified as the illness comes under control or goes into a full remission. People must accept that social malaise and being unhappy, or simply feeling out of sorts, are not necessarily legitimate reasons for taking medicines.

The home should be cleared periodically of all medicines which are not currently being taken and especially if they are beyond the expiry date. When this is done some surprising hoards will be revealed! There is no doubt that people tend to hang on to old medicines in case they need them; but medicines go off with keeping, especially when they are not kept in cool, dry, dark conditions. Drug hoarding is a potentially hazardous activity and is not necessary for older people in the United Kingdom because they are exempt from all prescription charges. If an old person cannot manage to organize his own pill-taking, help from a relative or neighbour will be required, for whom it may be necessary to keep complete control of the drugs.

18

Coping with disability

Some illnesses, such as strokes, have an abrupt onset followed by a variable degree of recovery over the succeeding weeks or months. The object of rehabilitation is to maximize that recovery and then to enable the victim to lead an active and independent life despite any residual disabilities he or she may suffer. Other diseases, such as Parkinson's disease, are characterized by a progressive course at a variable rate, and the objects of rehabilitation are to avoid or at least delay incapacity, and to enable the patient to overcome such handicaps as have developed. Rehabilitation is therefore a vital part of the treatment of illness, and the physiotherapist, the occupational therapist, and the speech therapist are vital members of the health care team. It must be added that their expertise is not invariably necessary or readily available, and a great deal of rehabilitation is carried out by nurses, relatives, and by patients themselves. For example, the best treatment for the early stages of Parkinson's disease is to walk a mile a day. Every activity is a therapeutic opportunity and will contribute towards the restoration and preservation of function – in other words, towards rehabilitation.

When we think of 'the disabled', the term seems to conjure up a romantic vision of youthful stoicism in the face of mutilating wounds sustained during feats of military or sporting heroism as typified by the late Group Captain Douglas Bader. It is true that there is a considerable burden of disability borne by the young, some of it of traumatic origin. The majority of disabled persons, however, are elderly, and have become disabled through the less glamorous ravages of disease. In fact, it is reckoned that 60 per cent of disabled persons are over 65 and that by the age of 75, 33 per cent of those living at home are disabled. The common disabilities and their main causes are listed in Table 17, and only problems of mobility and limb function will be considered here in any detail since impairment of the special senses, loss of speech and incontinence are dealt with elsewhere (see Table 17). There are of course

Table 17   *Common disabilities*

Disability	Causes	Examples
Instability (see also Chapter 11)	environmental	'trip and slip' especially if vision poor
	unsteadiness dizziness faint turns	exaggerated by drugs occasionally due to ear disease fall in blood pressure or abnormal heart beat
	locomotor	stroke arthritis Parkinson's disease amputation painful feet fractured femur
Immobility (see also Chapter 11)	locomotor visual breathlessness pain	as under 'instability' as under 'visual impairment' chronic heart or lung disease angina claudication arthritis
Upper limb		stroke arthritis multiple sclerosis
Deafness (see Chapter 13)		presbycusis wax otosclerosis
Visual impairment (see Chapter 13)		cateract glaucoma macular degeneration diabetes
Urinary incontinence (see Chapter 12)		stroke other brain disease prostatic disease prolapse infection senile vaginitis
Speech (see Chapter 11)		stroke
Social	communication personal relationships	speech or deafness depression phobias anxiety confusion

innumerable degrees of disability presenting a continuous spectrum from mild restriction of activity to the totally dependent bedfast condition, and one of the landmarks which represents a comparatively mild level of infirmity is the housebound state.

Being housebound

Rather less than a third of people over the age of 80 are effectively housebound, although it is impossible to give an exact figure since we are not dealing with an all-or-none phenomenon and appreciable numbers of people, for example, stay at home during the winter months but venture forth during better weather. Why are so many people housebound? The causes are many and several different factors are often involved, but they usually include one or more of the following:

Limited mobility (see Table 17)
Liability to fall (see Table 17)
Poor vision
Incontinence
Psychological factors, such as depression, anxiety

A distinction should be made between these underlying difficulties and the event which precipitates withdrawal from the outside world. In many cases it would appear that something has happened which has significantly altered the subject's perception of herself, so that she now regards herself as old and frail. Examples of such events include falling over in a public place, bereavement, a spell in hospital, or being mugged or merely insulted. And how do you cope when you are housebound? It becomes necessary to have the shopping delivered, or to get someone to do it for you — a relative, a neighbour, or the home help. A likely sequel is loneliness, which may be partially assuaged by attendance at an over-60s club, a luncheon club, or a social day centre, if transport can be arranged.

Inability to cope with household chores

The next level of disability is difficulty in managing the housework and cooking. Restricted mobility and poor vision are once again often to

169

blame, and it will be readily appreciated that someone who is unable to move about without hanging on to a frame, or a couple of sticks, or bits of furniture, with both hands, will find it impossible to cook or even wash up. Weakness or deformity of the upper limb will also render cooking and housework extremely laborious. The task of keeping the house clean is often carried out by relatives, even if the handicapped person lives alone, but failing that, the services of a home help three or four times a week should be sufficient. Meals on wheels should be available most weekdays, and some imaginative local authorites run a 'cook a meal' scheme whereby a neighbour is paid to cook an extra portion when she is catering for her own family and deliver it on a tray. All these services (see Chapter 4) are 'prosthetic' (replacement) rather than 'therapeutic' — enabling the client to perform the task herself. Many people would much prefer to do so, and there is a wide range of gadgets devised to circumvent some of the problems we have been discussing. Some of them are depicted in Fig. 12.

Severely reduced mobility: being wheelchair-bound

Even when the ability to walk usefully has been lost, dignity and an independent existence can be maintained in one's own home if the arms and hands retain their function. This makes it possible to transfer between bed, wheelchair, and toilet, and also permits operation of the self-propelled type of wheelchair. Electric models are also available, which can be controlled by a single knob and these are very helpful where one arm is affected and the other insufficiently powerful to propel a onesided chair. This kind of chair can help to make life worthwhile for those who have only made partial recoveries from their strokes.

People with severe arthritis affecting both hips may become completely fixed and incapable of any movement of these joints. It does not require a great feat of the imagination to appreciate that this makes the process of rising from a chair laborious and hazardous, and a 'spring-lift' (or 'ejector') seat may be required. Once up, some of these patients get about with the help of a frame, but others are unable to do so and become wheelchair-bound. Life is more difficult for them than for those with one good leg to bear their weight while transferring. Often, however, the arms are both fully functional. In any event, numerous adaptations around the home are likely to be needed so that kitchen and bathroom activities can be carried out at wheelchair level.

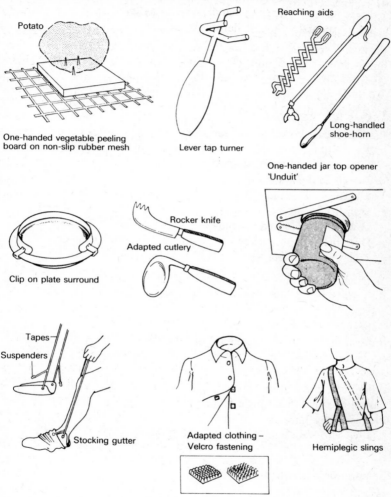

Fig. 12. Aids to daily living. (Reproduced from Coni, Davison, and Webster, *Lecture notes in geriatrics* 2nd edn (1980), with the kind permission of Blackwell Scientific Publications, Oxford.)

Difficulty with basic activities of self-care

The basic activities of self-care include washing, feeding, dressing and toileting oneself. Depending on help from others during meals or on the lavatory is particularly injurious to the pride, but may become inevitable through a combination of immobility, loss of use of one or both upper limbs, and loss of vision. Once again, there are devices to make these tasks possible (see Fig. 12), and the community occupational therapist can advise about these and about various adaptations to the home. Here are a few examples of the latter:

Grab-rails — lavatory, bathroom, stairs
Raised toilet seat
Chair and bed height adjusted
Ramps to replace steps
Electric sockets raised 1 m (3 feet) from floor
Stair lift
Lever taps (coloured red/blue)
Door bell, telephone bell wired to flashing lights for the deaf
Toilet-paper holder with serrated edge for one-handed tearing

Disability to this degree may well necessitate frequent attention from others in connection with the normal bodily functions, and after a period of six months this will qualify for the *attendance allowance*. Repeated or prolonged attention at night or continual supervision in order to avoid danger to oneself or others also qualifies. The allowance is tax-free and non-means-tested and the weekly rates as from November 1982 are £26.25 per day and night attendance or £17.50 for one or the other. The *invalid care allowance* (currently £19.70 a week, taxable) is payable to men and single women of working age who cannot work because they have to stay at home to look after a severely disabled relative who is receiving an attendance allowance.

Some specific problems

Mobility

A short leg, due to hip disease or a fractured thighbone (femur), leads to a limping gait putting the ball of the foot but not the toe to the ground, and may ultimately damage the spine. A built-up heel will help to correct the gait. A walking stick of the correct height can relieve the affected leg of 50 per cent of the weight of the body, and if it is attached by a wrist strap the hand is liberated for other uses when not actually walking. Those who are more crippled often find two sticks necessary, while those who have partially recovered from strokes derive greater support from a quadrupod. The Zimmer walking frame is extremely useful if both hands are strong enough to grip it, and it can be fitted with carrying basket; many hardy souls use them in the streets having overcome an initial reluctance to accept such an obvious badge of infirmity. Indoors, the walking frame can be rather unwieldy in confined spaces cluttered with furniture. About 60 per cent of stroke survivors manage to get about with one or other of these aids — half of the others walk unaided, and half do not walk at all.

Falls

Sometimes a great deal can be done for people who suffer repeated falls (see Chapter 11), but others are completely beyond medical treatment and live alone at considerable risk, especially if unable to get up from the floor. These people can be greatly helped by one of the many alarm call systems now available. A miniature radio transmitter is carried on the person and the touch of a button alerts a control centre which contacts a relative or neighbour, or, if there is no reply, one of the emergency services. One system activates the wearer's telephone which then tries a series of numbers in order to summon help.

Speech

Profound speech defects occasionally persist indefinitely after a stroke, but stroke clubs can do much to foster communication despite this handicap. They are usually self-help ventures, but can generally be located through the hospital speech therapist.

Deafness

Ideas to consider in addition to hearing aids include amplifiers for the television and receiving headsets with dual earpieces for the telephone (see Chapter 13). There are also communicators for the profoundly deaf in which the speaker talks into the microphone and the

173

deaf person wears or holds the earpiece, and these can be extremely effective.

Availability of aids and appliances

Unfortunately, aids and appliances are supplied through a bewildering variety of channels.

(1) *The British Red Cross Society*, through its local branches, lends commodes, bedpans, urinals, and sometimes wheelchairs.
(2) *The social services department of the local authority* supplies items of a non-nursing nature in connection with mobility and kitchen activities. It is responsible for compiling a register of disabled people under the Chronically Sick and Disabled Persons Act of 1970 but refusal to be entered on this register does not disqualify from assistance of a financial or practical nature. The department employs domiciliary occupational therapists and social workers, and provides a range of supportive home services.
(3) *The district health authority* provdes aids to home nursing like incontinence sheets and pads and ripple mattresses, and is responsible for running the *community nursing service.*
(4) *The Department of Health and Social Security*, through the local *Artificial Limb and Appliance Centre*, supplies wheelchairs, mobile chairs, and accessories.
(5) *The family doctor* or the *hospital consultant* prescribe medical and surgical appliances.

Further information may be obtained from the addresses listed in the appendix, and it is well worth seeking advice from the local branch of Age Concern, or the Citizens' Advice Bureau.

19

Death and bereavement

All good things must come to an end and life is no exception. Birth presupposes death and even if we run successfully the gauntlet of life ageing guarantees mortality. Everyone's philosophy should embrace both the prospect and the reality of death. The death of a loved one is one of the most stressful of life's events; the pain of the loss is the price we pay for the joy and security of love. Premature death is most distressing of all and is to be avoided if possible, but as the prerogative of the elderly death can be seen to be a good thing. Death after a long, full and well-lived life is a natural consummation and the old person usually sees it in that light.

In the earlier part of this century death at younger ages was commonplace and was often caused by an infection, such as pneumonia, typhoid fever or tuberculosis. Improved nutrition, water supply, sewage disposal and housing have so reduced the incidence of these diseases that in England in 1982, 78 per cent of all deaths occurred in those aged 65 years or more (Fig. 13); the major causes being heart disease, cancer, stroke and lung infection. Doctors are almost always involved in the care of the dying; indeed the authors regard this as an important part of their work.

Telling the patient

The question 'Am I going to die, doctor?' is often in the patient's mind for weeks or months before death. Sometimes it is not put into words, and if it is, the person asked may not be the doctor, but a relative, a friend, or someone else who happens to be visiting. It is possible that the doctor is regarded as too busy or too remote a figure to be consulted. It is possible too that the patient might wish to avoid embarrassing the doctor who up to this time has been talking hopefully about recovery from illness, or it may be that the patient would rather not have his

175

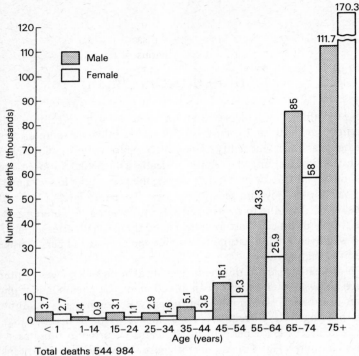

Total deaths 544 984
Deaths age 65 and over, 78 per cent; age 75 and over 52 per cent

Fig. 13. Age at death, England 1983. (OCPS data.)

suspicions confirmed at this stage. Certainly some doctors and patients appear to be too embarrassed to discuss death and will brush aside any direct approach, perhaps with a gentle rebuke.

If, however, there is a good doctor–patient relationship, discussion of these matters should not be too difficult. When the question 'Am I going to die, doctor?' is put, then the doctor should answer simply, giving the patient a clear indication of what is happening, but avoiding medical complexity, jargon and unnecessary doubts and fears. Many aver that listening to the patient, as opposed to telling him things, is even more important at this stage of his illness; evasion of the fundamental issue cannot be expected to earn the patient's confidence.

176

However, not all patients wish to be given 'the whole truth and nothing but the truth', and the detailed discussion that is most helpful to one person might be a psychological disaster to another. When death is imminent the patient is usually oblivious of his plight, or sometimes is so overwhelmed by symptoms, such as breathlessness, in urgent need of relief, that the question ('Am I dying?') is simply not put. Prior to that the patient's main anxiety tends to be less about dying than about his current and seemingly intractable symptoms.

It is important for those concerned in the care of the dying not to see death as a wholly negative and undesirable phenomenon or as some sort of 'medical failure'. This would be unrealistic and likely to cause embarrassment to all parties. A positive, hopeful encouraging approach is required and while no-one would wish to burden the dying person with unwelcome facts, information requested should not lightly be withheld. When patients are dying it is usually better for the patient himself, the close relatives and the doctor to speak simply and honestly one with another. This is no time for lies or charades and the deliberate avoidance of the central issue. A failure to be honest and openly communicative can so easily leave the patient anxious, frustrated, resentful, and suffering unnecessary distress.

A positive approach to dying

Once it is realized that the end is in sight, that the disease is incurable, and that heroic measures are no longer indicated, it is important for all those concerned to have a clear understanding of their positive roles to play. The dying patient has the role of continuing to live and enjoying life in as much as he is able while at the same time manifestly dying. Surprisingly, life can still be worth living even while dying, as many terminal cancer patients testify. Interests in family, friends and surroundings should be maintained yet at the same time the patient has to prepare to leave them all.

The relatives and friends need to have some estimate of the time-scale of the events leading up to death; they have the complementary roles of living their own lives while supporting the patient, and yet allowing him to withdraw from them. The duration of the terminal phase can be measured in days, weeks or months, depending on circumstances. Knowledge of the likely duration helps the relatives in the organization

177

of their time in support of the patient. It also allows planning of a programme of care at home or in hospital; often both are used. Doctors, nurses and social workers have to use their special knowledge, technical skills and understanding to provide some relief for the more severe physical and mental distresses. This enabling approach to dying is the key to a good death. Euthanasia literally means a gentle and easy death and is, in this context, usually achievable (see below, p. 181).

A place to die

Most people, knowing that they are soon to die, express a preference for remaining in their own homes if at all possible. This wish should be respected and many relatives are both able and willing to provide the level of support to allow this to occur. However, there is a trend towards death in hospital or nursing home with only about a third of deaths occurring in the dying person's own home or in the home of a relative or friend (Table 18). The reason for the trend towards dying in institutions

Table 18 *Place of death, all causes (England and Wales, 1982, OPCS†
data)*

Place	Percentages	
	Male	Female
NHS Hospitals	58	59
(includes psychiatric)	(1.7)	(2.3)
All other institutions	5	12
Deceased person's home	30	24
Other person's home	7	5

† Total deaths: 290 166 males, 291 695 females

is not because relatives are callous and uncaring, but because the amount of care needed by the aged patient cannot be provided by the (often equally aged) relatives and friends; even the children may be well past retirement age.

Sometimes admission to hospital is requested in the belief that it will be much better for the patient. But this is not always so. Admission can result in less care, in terms of personal contact, because one nurse may be caring for half a dozen patients, whereas the patient at home may have the sole attention of one or more relatives. All too often the patient has little choice because the burden of home care overwhelms the relatives. Disturbed nights and a great deal of physical effort, although tolerable in the short term, may be unbearable if prolonged. In cases of difficulty, support from the local authority or voluntary services is very important and may tip the balance in favour of care at home, for example someone to sit with the patient to allow the relative time to go shopping or to keep vigil to allow the relatives to sleep.

Pre-death dependence

Terminal care for elderly people can be quite prolonged, for months and even years. During this time physical deterioration with decreasing mobility and possibly mental disturbance and persistent incontinence is to be anticipated. Continuing home care for these cases requires strongly supportive relatives, careful management and a great deal of help from the domiciliary health and social services. Help can also be obtained from private nursing or domestic service agencies. For cancer cases there are specialist organizations, such as the Marie Curie organization (see appendix). The social worker, health visitor or community nursing sister can usually enlist help from these agencies, if required.

Too early admission to hospital for terminal care is to be avoided on humanitarian grounds because most dying people prefer to be at home, but also because the hospital service simply could not cope with all demands if very long periods of pre-death care were freely offered. Sometimes a short spell in hospital for the relatives' respite, and a revision of the drug treatment to control the patient's symptoms, is all that is necessary to allow home care to continue. The essence of the matter is for help to be mobilized in such a way that all parties (the carers and the cared for) receive appropriate support with due regard to both their emotional and their physical needs.

Social needs of relatives

Restriction of social life is surprisingly well tolerated by relatives who with love and devotion care for the sick at home. However it is important that relief from stress is available from time to time, if they are not to crack under the strain. It is especially important that they have adequate sleep and can maintain some social life outside the home.

Ageing: the facts

Equally it is important not to relieve relatives of their burden unnecessarily.

It requires a judicious use of resources to give the best overall support to the many families in need with due regard to all the psychological, social and physical problems. Most want to care for their elderly folk and may well feel guilty if they do not. However, unless sufficient help is given to relatives they may have to abdicate their responsibilities altogether and as a result suffer great emotional turmoil; inevitably the patient will suffer too. Regular rest periods for the relatives by having the elderly person admitted to hospital for a week or two at a time can be arranged, if necessary. If death appears imminent, admission is best cancelled and the patient allowed to die peacefully at home. Death on the way to hospital or very soon after admission is most distressful to all concerned, especially when it comes at the end of a lengthy struggle to manage at home.

Additionally relatives and helpers need to have answers to questions such as 'What should I do if he gets an attack of pain?' or, 'supposing she dies while I am in the room or when a neighbour is visiting?' These are all possible reasons for anxiety and each one must be dealt with in turn. Mostly, the answers are straightforward but by discussing the problems anxiety may be allayed to the extent that the sick person may achieve his wish and be allowed to remain at home.

Feelings of inadequacy in the relatives or neighbours are a common reason for requesting admission to hospital. Yet, as explained earlier, in many cases the relatives and neighbours can offer a much better standard of care than can the hospital because the main need is for love and sympathetic understanding, together with help with simple household tasks and personal care, including bathing, feeding, and toilet, rather than for medical and nursing expertise. Additionally intimate knowledge of the patient's likes and dislikes is something which relatives and friends may possess but cannot be expected of the nurse or doctor. However, specialist tasks will have to be dealt with by the professionals, such as the giving of a pain-relieving injection or the insertion of a catheter in a patient with loss of urinary control.

Social needs of the patient

When arrangements are being made for home care for the dying the family doctor and those working with him will be able to advise on details of management. The importance of simple practical help cannot be overemphasized; but care for the patient must also have a social content. Time hangs heavy on those who are housebound. Just to have someone in the house to talk to or to pop in on an informal basis can transform the situation for a sick old person at home because loneliness, boredom or insecurity greatly aggravate the symptoms of any illness. If a relative living near can be available then usually that is the best arrangement. If relatives are not available because they work or live at a distance, to have someone else popping in gives enormous relief, not just to the sick person, but to the relatives too.

When death is near the dying person must not be left alone. Relatives and close friends can arrange to be at the bedside on a rota basis. Unless the patient strongly objects, the parish priest should always be informed.

Euthanasia

Since the illnesses causing death are often mentally and physically distressful as well as protracted, it is understandable that many would wish to avoid the later stages. They urge that the law be changed to allow those who wish for a swift, merciful release from prolonged and useless suffering to have their lives terminated and to be able to secure the necessary medical help to achieve this. The Voluntary Euthanasia Society founded in 1935 exists to promote legislation which would permit an adult person, suffering from a severe illness for which no relief is known, to receive an immediate painless death, if and only if, that is their expressed wish (see appendix).

However, euthanasia as a form of medically assisted suicide bristles with ethical as well as legal problems, and there seems little likelihood of it becoming legal in Britain in the foreseeable future. The authors believe that the majority of medical practitioners would not wish to see themselves cast in the role of executioner. On the other hand, medical treatment to secure a gentle and easy death when death already is approaching naturally (as opposed to killing to avoid a long and miserable terminal illness) is surely a part of good medical practice. It is the doctor's vocation to cure sometimes, to relieve often, and to comfort always, even in death.

181

The death

When elderly people die, they may be drowsy or unconscious for hours or even days before the end comes. When the death is imminent breathing will probably become slower and more shallow, and possibly intermittent, until it stops altogether. After the death the doctor should quickly be informed by the relative so that the death can be confirmed and the death certificate issued, and thereafter contact should be made with the clergyman and funeral director and also with the patient's solicitor. If, as often happens, the spouse or nearest relative of the deceased is very frail or is too upset another relative, friend or neighbour, should be asked to make the necessary arrangements. A social worker may be needed to help with claims for insurance, death grant, pension, and so forth, and in many cases will already be well known to the family.

Bereavement

The loss of a loved one through death inevitably arouses strong emotional feelings, especially anxiety, fear, anger and sorrow. These grief reactions are normal and need to be expressed to others to make real the loss. Left alone with no-one to talk to, or no-one willing to listen, the bereaved person feels extremely isolated and may imagine he is going out of his mind.

Normal grief reactions occur in recognizable stages: shock and numbness; anger, resentment, pining and sorrow; and eventually, resolution. It takes time for the sequence to be worked through and the processes of mourning should be encouraged by friends and relatives to allow the stage of resolution to be reached (Table 19). The pain of the loss has to be faced fair and square. Attempts to stifle feelings, to ignore the loss

Table 19   *Coping with grief*

Face the loss directly and do not isolate yourself.
Discuss your feelings readily with relatives and friends.
Do not 'blot out' your feelings with drugs or alcohol.
Allow grief to progress naturally, neither hurry nor stifle it.
Relatives are not to regard the bereft as ill, in need of protection or of 'cheering up'.

182

or to rush through the period of grief to get it all over and done with may well result in later emotional and even physical illness.

Medical help is frequently requested by close relatives early in bereavement to relieve the anxiety, depression and insomnia. Short-term use of sleeping tablets and tranquillisers may be needed but they should be used only for a short time and never to 'blot out' normal grief.

Old age is a time of loss (see Chapter 3), and a good sound net-work of social contacts is essential at this time to help one cope with multiple losses. Yet so often people go it alone in late life because they have not positively cultivated their friendships especially in late middle age. The development of personal and lasting friendships is yet another way in which illness may be minimized in old age.

Some legal implications of incapacity

Power of attorney. When the elderly person is mentally capable he may if he wishes appoint some other person to manage his affairs; in other words, he grants the power of attorney. This legal right to act for another is quickly arranged through a solicitor and for a patient incapaci-tated by physical (but not mental) illness it is the obvious solution to some of the practical problems, such as the purchase of goods or the payment of bills. If the patient's mind fails then the agent previously legally appointed is no longer able to act legally. The law is so designed to protect the interests of the mentally ill.

It is important for doctors, relatives and solicitors to be absolutely clear about this point of law: 'Where such a change occurs to the principal (patient) that he can no longer act for himself, the agent whom he has appointed can no longer act for him'. (Lord Justice Brett, 1897.)

Court of protection. If the patient, because of mental incapacity, cannot manage his own affairs then it is necessary to apply to the Court of Protection (see appendix). In most cases a Receiver will be appointed to act as the patient's agent; usually an interested relative or some other suitable person. When the assets are small the appointment of a Receiver may not be necessary but the realization by the patient that his property is being protected by the Court often removes a source of worry. The

Court will require an appropriate medical certificate completed by the doctor to state the nature and severity of the illness together with the likely prognosis.

Most of the work of the Court of Protection is to do with elderly people, especially those with a dementing illness. The powers of the Receiver are strictly controlled; for example, he may not on his own initiative make loans or gifts or dispose of any property or investments but he can and should see to it that the patient is provided with those little extras that add so much flavour to life, such as special foods, drinks, flowers, toilet articles and clothing.

20

A glimpse into the future

We have seen how western societies can anticipate a substantial increase in the number of 'old old' — those in their late 70s and in particular those in their 80s and 90s. We have also seen that disease and disability is increasingly something that happens to the old, and that the incidence of many of the chronic physical and mental ills rises steeply among old people. From this picture, optimists have concluded that the elixir of eternal life is within reach and that we can look for a wonderful increase in the human lifespan*. The pessimists envisage a tremendous rise in the burden of long-term physical and mental dependency, of chronic illness, suffering and invalidism, imposing an intolerable strain on the sufferers, their families, and the resources of the health and social services. The realists are aware that there is a third scenario, arguably both more likely and more desirable than either of these.

Lifespans

The human lifespan shows very little sign of increasing at all significantly. What has changed, very fortunately, is that in the affluent countries, the large (and increasing) majority of us are fulfilling it, so that life expectation at birth has certainly risen a great deal, although that at age 65 or 70 has scarcely risen at all. There may be a lot more octogenarians around and quite a few more centenarians, † but people do not seem to be showing much sign of living beyond 115, at least in those countries whose records are reliable. The proportions of 65-year-old men and women who can expect to live to 100 are still only one in 1000 and five in 1000 respectively. It seems to be agreed that the human lifespan is about 85 or 90 at best and is likely to remain so, which is a considerable improvement on 30 or even 20 years ago.

The progressive elimination of infantile, childhood, and premature

†The number of congratulatory messages from the Queen to UK citizens on reaching their hundredth birthdays has risen steadily from 200 in 1952 to 1750 in 1982!

adult mortality, taken in conjunction with a fixed lifespan of 85 years give or take a few either way, has implications best illustrated graphically by what are known as survival curves (Fig. 14). Mankind, in recent years

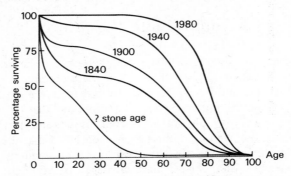

Fig. 14. Survival curves. United States. (Source: US Bureau of Health Statistics.)

and in the western world, is the first and only species to rejoice in the happy expectation of entering the world with an excellent chance of surviving until the end of his natural life. Primitive man, like wild animals, is, from the moment of his birth, subject to the random depredations of disease, trauma, famine, and predators, so that there is a constant rate of attrition of a given cohort. This situation has been compared to the fate of a batch of glass tumblers purchased by a self-service cafeteria (Fig. 15), and which are thereafter haphazardly destroyed by customers and washing-up staff until none remain. Such a population is scarcely permitted to exhibit the phenomenon of senescence, although even those few stone-age men who attained a good age presumably became physically feebler, and even cafeteria glasses, if badly chipped, become more prone to breakage. The perfectly random survival curve shows a constant rate of mortality (e.g. 50 per cent per unit time). As civilization advances, the environmental hazards are progressively brought under control, and an intermediate phase (see Fig. 14) shows a high attrition rate during the vulnerable period of infancy, a low but continued mortality during adolescence and early adult life, mainly from the infectious diseases, and a further increased mortality during the second period of vulnerability — late middle and

186

A glimpse into the future

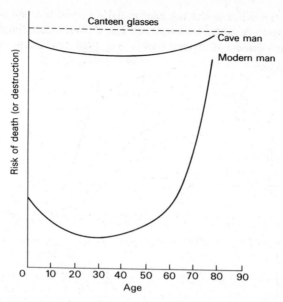

Fig. 15. Senescence as an increasing risk (diagrammatic).

old age. If present trends continue, and we shall explore the probability that they will do so, mortality rates will become negligible during infancy, childhood, adolescence, and adulthood, and will only become appreciable at the end of the lifespan — when they will be enormous. This phenomenon has been called 'the rectangularization of the survival curve', for reasons which are obvious from a glance at Fig. 14.

The effects of health education and preventive medicine

Campaigns to promote health have achieved considerable success in the United States and, perhaps to a lesser extent, in the United Kingdom. The avowed object is the prevention of certain major diseases, notably lung cancer and cardiovascular diseases such as stroke and coronary heart disease. It remains questionable whether a realistic goal is total prevention, or merely delaying the progress, of these killing diseases, so that their effects are postponed into old age. Perhaps the point is an

187

academic one, since either achievement would be desirable. Those who believe that healthy habits postpone but do not offer freedom from degenerative disease of the arteries will point to the findings of published series of post-mortem examinations of subjects dying in their 90s, who have been found to have advanced and widespread atheroma. Those who feel that the consequences of this process can be avoided altogether will quote the evidence that stroke disease and myocardial infarction ('coronary thrombosis') have both started to decline as a cause of death in the United States and, to a lesser extent, the United Kingdom. They will also emphasize that cancer of the lung, another of the great killers, is almost completely avoidable.

It is perhaps worth stating once again the simple rules for a long and vigorous life:

(1) No *smoking* — and this almost certainly applies to marijuana too.
(2) *Alcohol* in moderation or not at all.
(3) Do not become significantly *overweight*, and adhere to a diet containing sparse quantities of meat, dairy products, and polyunsaturated animal fats in general, relying on high-fibre carbohydrate foods for your staple diet. The prudent diet is based on vegetables (especially pulses), fruit, cereals and cereal products (e.g. porridge and wholemeal bread). Of the meats, dry poultry such as turkey is relatively harmless. It is perhaps worth mentioning that fatty fish such as mackerel may even protect against atherosclerosis. Eskimos still living on their traditional diet of fish, and recycled fish in the form of seal, walrus, whale and bear seem to remain totally free of coronary artery disease and other arterial disorders — and appear to have a regular bowel habit as well!
(4) In youth or middle age, if you suffer from a *high blood pressure*, this should be effectively treated.
(5) In *retirement*, remain socially and economically active, retaining a sense of usefulness and purpose.
(6) *Throughout life*, maintain a high level of physical activity and fitness.
(7) It helps to choose your parents!

The compression of morbidity

If the elimination of some of the great killing diseases is a genuine

188

possibility, what will we die of? We will die because we will reach the end of our lives. We have seen in Chapter 16 that the hallmark of extreme old age and fraility is homeostatic incompetence, so that we lose the ability to maintain a constant internal environment in terms of its physical and chemical properties in the face of an external challenge. It takes a smaller and smaller insult to knock us off our perches. It may be influenza, or it may be an accident or some apparently trivial event that finally sends the system haywire. When a warm-blooded organism loses its homeostatic mechanisms, it become unviable.

The implications of this are much more important than mere prolongation of life. The disappearing diseases, if so prematurely optimistic a term may be used, are those that do not merely kill, but which often kill slowly and lead to a prolonged period of disability and dependency — a kind of pre-death twilight which may last many months or years. The kind of death we are predicting is one in which the final illness lasts hours or days. The conclusions we draw are that we can look forward to a future in which premature death is virtually eliminated, we all live our allotted span (nearer to four-score years and ten than three-score and ten) in health and vigour and then die after a mercifully brief and final illness. This ideal, unfortunately, can never be fully attained because we will continue to destroy ourselves and each other with our motor bikes, our wars, our narcotics, and our faulty lifestyles. But we do seem to be getting the message, and the compression of morbidity seems to be a likely trend in the affluent societies of the western world. Old people are, it seems, fitter than they used to be.

Senile dementia

There is one great spanner in this elysian works, and that is senile dementia (see Chapter 10). This disease causes more severe disability than any other because it is more completely destructive of the capacity to sustain an independent existence over a period of many months or years than any other. It has often been shown that it is mental rather than physical frailty that is the biggest single factor necessitating institutional care. So far, we have very little idea how this disorder may be prevented. There is little real evidence that continued use of the intellect offers any protection against it, although one instinctively feels that this must be of some value in its own right. It should be remembered that the other main variety of failure of the brain in old age is that due to arterial disease, and that it is therefore reasonable to hope that its incidence will diminish as we adopt a more health-conscious lifestyle. And as we saw in Chapter 10, these two diseases of the brain coexist in a considerable proportion of patients who will also clearly fare better if the atherosclerotic element can be modified or avoided.

The dependent elderly

It is conventional to anticipate a steady increase in the numbers of aged, physically and mentally infirm, very dependent individuals, whose lives are a burden to themselves, to their families, to the health and social services, and to the taxpayer. This chapter offers the alternative vision of a society in which there are about the same number of fit, active citizens in each decade up to the age of 70, followed by a steady decline in numbers thereafter due to illnesses of mercifully brief duration. Such a vision is only incompletely attainable since accidents and self-destructive habits will always be with us, but it nevertheless carries profound implications for society. Most of these implications are clearly desirable, but some of them present an exhilarating challenge — namely a far greater degree of integration of its older members into the mainstream of society, and the implementation of far more flexible retirement policies.

Looking forward

But this book is addressed to individuals more than to society as a whole, and for the individual, there is a great deal of encouragement to be drawn. Certain aspects of ageing cannot be modified and in the current state of our knowledge are unlikely to become modifiable. These include such cosmetic attributes as greying and thinning of hair and wrinkling of the skin, as well as rather more vital functions such as diminishing reserve of the kidneys and loss of elasticity of the lens of the eye. Other attributes often regarded as inevitably declining with age seem to be readily modified and sometimes improved by personal decisions, and these include exercise tolerance, muscular strength, and lung reserve, cardiac reserve, reaction time, short-term memory, social ability, systolic blood pressure, intelligence testing, and loss of bone. And

A glimpse into the future

perhaps most encouraging of all, there is a whole range of killing and disabling diseases which can be postponed or avoided altogether by these same personal decisions.

Ageing is something that affects us all, personally and through our families. Too many of us retain negative attitudes of gloom and despondency towards it. We should instead try to become better informed about it because, as we have seen, a positive and optimistic approach and continued high expectations can enable us to achieve the object of growing old successfully.

Useful addresses

United Kingdom

(Note that many of these organizations have local branches; and Citizens' Advice Bureaux are often very helpful)

Age Concern,
Bernard Sunley House,
60 Pitcairn Road,
Mitcham,
Surrey, CR4 3LL
01 640 5431
(contact with local organizations)

Alzheimer Disease Society,
(and local branches)
3rd Floor,
Bank Buildings,
Fulham Broadway,
London SW6 1EP
01 381 3177

Association of Carers,
(self-help, irrespective of disease or disability)
58 New Road,
Chatham,
Kent, ME4 4QR
0634 813981/2

British Nursing Association,
470 Oxford Street,
London W1N 0HQ
01 629 9030
(nursing agency)

192

Useful addresses

Chest, Heart and Stroke Association,
Tavistock House North,
Tavistock Square,
London WC1H 9SE
01 387 3012
(contact with local stroke clubs)

Counsel and Care for the Elderly,
131 Middlesex Street,
London E1 7JF
01 621 1624
(counselling, financial assistance)

Court of Protection,
(apply to Chief Clerk)
25 Store Street,
London WC1E 7BP
01 636 6877

CRUSE,
Cruse House,
126 Sheen Road,
Richmond,
Surrey TW9 1UR
01 940 4818
(counselling and advice to the widowed)

The Disabled Living Foundation,
346 Kensington High Street,
London W14 8NS
01 602 2491
(produces useful publications, including one or two on incontinence)

Marie Curie Memorial Foundation,
(apply to Welfare Official)
138 Sloane Street,
London SW1X 9AY
01 730 9157

National Council for Carers and their Elderly Dependants,
29 Chilworth Mews,
London W2 3RG
01 586 9844

Office of Population Censuses and Surveys (OPCS),
Segensworth Road,
Titchfield,
Fareham,
Hants, PO15 5RS
01 242 0262

Parkinson's Disease Society,
81 Queen's Road,
London SW19 8NR
01 946 2500
(booklets, local branches)

Registered Nursing Home Association,
7-7A Station Road,
Finchley,
London N3 2SB
01 346 1224
(list of nursing homes)

The Royal National Institute for the Blind,
224 Great Portland Street,
London W1N 6AA
01 388 1266

The Royal National Institute for the Deaf,
105 Gower Street,
London WC1E 6AH
01 387 8033

Social Trends
A useful review of official statistical information. Obtainable from booksellers, Government Bookshops (e.g. 49 High Holborn, London, WC1V 6HB) and, Open University Educational Enterprises Ltd., 12 Cofferidge Close, Stony Stratford, Milton Keynes, MK11 1BY (Tel: 0908 566744)

The University of the Third Age,
6 Parkside Gardens,
London SW19 5EY
01 947 0401

Useful addresses

The Voluntary Euthanasia Society,
13 Prince of Wales Terrace,
London W8 5PG
01 937 7770

United States

Action for Independent Maturity,
1909 K Street NW,
Washington DC 20048.

American Association of Retired Persons,
1909 K Street NW,
Washington DC 20049.
[Much useful information.]

American Health Care Association,
1200 15th Street MW,
Washington DC 20005.
[List recommended rest homes, etc.]

Gray Panthers,
3700 Chestnut Street,
Philadelphia PA 19104.
[Militant anti-ageism.]

National Association of Home Care,
205 C Street NE,
Washington DC 20002.

National Council of Senior Citizens,
1511 K Street NW,
Washington DC 20005.

Glossary

Anaemia: Reduction in concentration of haemoglobin in the blood (normal range: 13.5-18 g per 100 ml for men, 11.5-16.4 g per 100 ml for women).

Apnoea: Absence of breathing.

Atherosclerosis (atheroma, arteriosclerosis): Degenerative disease in which the arteries are narrowed by the patchy deposition of cholesterol round the interior of the wall.

Autoimmune: Immune response directed against the body's own tissues.

Blood pressure: The pressure within the arteries: *systolic* – during systole, or active cardiac contraction (the heart beat); *diastolic* – during diastole or the pause between beats.

Brain stem: Part of the central nervous system linking the brain with the spinal cord, and containing vital centres (e.g. respiratory centre). Destroyed in judicial hanging, modern concepts of death emphasize brain stem death as the most essential criterion.

Cancer: Malignant disease characterized by uncontrolled cell multiplication causing growths of abnormal tissue (tumours), often with daughter growths in distant sites (metastases or secondaries) due to cell migration.

Carbohydrate: Group of organic compounds of carbon, hydrogen and oxygen forming important constituents of the diet and including cellulose, starch, and sugars; ultimately broken down in gut to simple, single sugar molecules (monosaccharides, e.g. glucose) from original double (disaccharides, e.g. sucrose) or complex (polysaccharides) molecules.

Cerebral: Of or pertaining to the cerebrum, the higher part of the brain.

Cholesterol: Fatty compound having the formula $C_{27}H_{45}OH$ occurring in the plasma, mainly synthesized in the liver, and partly responsible for formation of atherosclerotic plaques; it occurs in the diet (e.g. egg yolk).

Chromosome: Thread of DNA (*q.v.*) which transmits genetic information; normally 23 pairs of chromosomes in the nucleus of each cell in the human; genes (*q.v.*) occupy set positions on the chromosome.

Collagen: The main supporting protein in the connective tissue of the body.

Colon: Large intestine.

Continuing care: The hospital care of patients so severely disabled that they will never enjoy sufficient recovery to return to their own home; also known as extended care; some confusion has arisen since the requisition of the term by the hospice movement to mean terminal care.

Cornea: Transparent front part of tough outer coat of eyeball.

Coronary arteries: The arteries carrying blood to supply the heart muscle (myocardium)

Cortex: Outer layer; in the case of the brain, comprises the so-called 'grey matter' containing the cell bodies, while the underlying 'white matter' consists of their fibres.

196

Glossary

Corticosteroids, steroids: Class of drugs derived from the hormones produced by the cortex of the adrenal gland, used for their powerful anti-inflammatory effect but also liable to produce numerous adverse effects.

Crude birth-rate: Births per 1000 population all ages.

Demography: Statistical data relating to populations.

Deoxyribonucleic acid (DNA): The carrier of genetic information; the molecule has a double helix configuration and each chain has information completely specifying the other chain.

Diabetes: Disease in which level of glucose in the blood is too high, so that significant quantities of sugar are also found in the urine; fasting level of over 8 mmol/l or a random reading over 11 mmol/l in the plasma establishes the diagnosis with reasonable certainty.

Diastolic: When the heart is relaxed and dilated, diastole of the heart alternates with systole (contraction).

Diuretic: Drug to increase the production of urine and thus disperse fluid (water, salt and potassium) in conditions such as heart failure.

Duodenum: The part of the small bowel which starts at the exit of the stomach and curves around the pancreas. It is liable to ulceration when the acid secretion of the stomach is excessive.

Electrolyte: Simple inorganic compounds existing in ionic form in solution (e.g. sodium, chloride, potassium).

Embolus, embolism: The detachment of a blood clot, either from a vein to pass through the heart to the lungs, or from the left heart to pass through the arteries to reach the brain, leg, or other destination.

Enzyme: A protein which catalyses (aids) a biochemical reaction.

Fibroblasts: Fibre-producing cells of connective tissue forming the supporting and binding tissues throughout the body.

Gene: The basic unit of heredity, carried on the chromosome (*q.v.*). The primary action of the gene is to synthesize a specific protein. Each gene controls a particular inherited characteristic to the individual. Genes, like the chromosomes, are paired.

Genetic: Concerning genes or origins.

Genetic code: System of storage of genetic information (as genes) on chromosomes.

Genetic mutation: A permanent transmissible change in the genetic material; gives rise to heritable variation.

Genetics: Science of heredity.

General fertility rate: Births per 1000 females aged 15–44.

Genome: The complete set of hereditary factors contained in the genes and chromosomes and obtained from the germ cells – ovum and sperm from mother and father respectively.

Goitre: Swelling of the thyroid gland.

Habituation: A condition resulting from continued use of a drug with desire to continue its use even though there may be detrimental effects to the individual.

197

Ageing: the facts

Haemorrhoids: Swelling of the veins (varicosities) in and around the anus, may bleed; also called piles.

Health visitor: A highly qualified and experienced nurse whose main function is to advise on health matters, especially prevention; initially they were involved entirely with mothers and babies but are beginning to take a greater interest in the problems of the elderly.

Hernia: Protrusion of intestine or other tissue through some abnormal opening, especially through wall of abdomen (abdominal hernia), commonly called a rupture.

Hiatus hernia: A common condition, seldom serious, in which part of the stomach lies above the diaphragm in the chest, exposing the oesophagus (gullet) to stomach acid, sometimes causing indigestion, bleeding, or even narrowing (stricture) of the oesophagus.

Hodgkin's disease: A malignant disease with progressive anaemia, enlargement of lymph glands and spleen.

Homeostasis: The ability to maintain a constant internal physical and chemical environment despite variations in the external environment.

Hormone: A chemical substance produced in the body which regulates the activity of other tissues or organs, e.g. thyroxine from thryoid gland and insulin from the pancreas.

Hypnotic: A sedative drug used in order to promote sleep.

Infarction: Death of an organ or part of an organ usually due to completely or partially cut off blood supply: *infarct* – the zone of tissue so affected, *or* the clinical occurrence.

Intracranial: Within the skull or cranium; e.g. involving the brain.

Ischaemia: Damage to an organ or part of an organ whose blood supply is insufficient.

Lean body mass: The fat-free mass of the body; excludes metabolically inactive storage fat.

Leukaemia: Malignant disease of white blood cells; classified on basis of cell type and speed of onset.

Lifespan: Age at which average individual would die if there were no premature disease or accidents; for man, about 85-90.

Lipids: Fatty substances.

Lipofuscin: Granules with characteristic staining properties found in cells in many tissues especially in the elderly, for example nervous tissue, muscle, liver and kidney.

Maximum life potential: Age at death of longest-lived member of species; for man – 115 years.

Mechanoreceptor: Specialized tissue sensitive to mechanical pressure distortion and able to signal (via the nervous system) such distortions; detects pressure, movement, and sound.

Metabolism: Chemical processes of the body; *catabolism* is the process of breaking down complex substances into simple ones, and *anabolism* is the process whereby complex molecules, particularly proteins, are synthesized from nutrients.

Micturition: The act of passing urine.

Glossary

Mutant: A new form resulting from (genetic) mutation (*q.v*).

Myocardial infarction: Death of part of heart muscle (myocardium) due to inadequate blood flow through coronary arteries.

Neurone: Nerve cell, and its appendages, e.g. within brain or spinal cord; these cells, unlike most other tissue, are not renewed throughout life, and if destroyed, are not replaced.

Neurotransmitter: Chemical substance, normally an amine, which transmits the nervous impulse from one neurone to another.

Osteoarthritis: Degenerative disease affecting joints.

Osteoporosis: Diminution in mass of bone, leading to greater risk of fracture.

Packed cell volume (pcv) (haematocrit): Proportion of volume of blood occupied by red cells, measured after centrifugation to pack the cells at the bottom of the tube and leave clear plasma above them.

Pancreas: Large gland behind the stomach which releases insulin into the blood stream and various digestive enzymes into the duodenum.

Parameter: A variable which we measure to determine a quantity or function which is not directly measurable, e.g. pulse rate and blood pressure as a guide to heart action or blood sugar as a guide to insulin action.

Paranoia: Mental derangement with hallucinations and delusions of persecution.

Pituitary gland: Small ductless gland at base of brain which by hormones regulates many other hormone-producing (endocrine) glands, e.g. thyroid and adrenals; often referred to as 'conductor of the endocrine orchestra'.

Psychosis: Severe mental derangement.

Psychotropic: Applied to drugs that affect the mental state.

Rectum: Final part of large intestine where faecal material from the colon is stored until evacuated via the anus.

Renal: Appertaining to the kidney.

Ribonucleic acid (RNA): Transmits information from the DNA (*q.v.*) to the protein-forming (including enzymes) systems of the cell.

Senescence: A progressive loss of physiological adaptability to the environment due to ageing and culminating in death; the process or condition of growing old.

Stroke: The effect of a sudden disturbance of the blood supply to a part of the brain.

Systolic: When the heart is contracted; systole of the heart alternates with diastole (relaxation).

Third age: Phase of active retirement (first age – childhood and adolescence; second age – employment and rearing a family; fourth age – frailty and dependency).

Thyroid: Endocrine (i.e. hormone-secreting) gland situated in the neck below the larynx and producing the hormone thyroxine which regulates metabolism; *thyrotoxicosis, hyperthyroidism* – overactivity of the gland; *myxoedema, hypothyroidism* – underactivity of the gland.

Virus: Agent very much smaller than bacteria and invisible with the ordinary microscope, which may cause disease (influenza, poliomyelitis, measles, chickenpox, mumps).

Index

Index

Index

gastritis 121
general practitioner 28
geriatirc medicine 30
Gerovital 52
giant cell arteritis 154
Ginseng 52
glaucoma 113
glyceryl trinitrate 134
'going off' 147-57
gold 92
Gompertz, Benjamin 37
gout 93
grief
    coping with 182-3
    reactions 182

habituation, to drugs 162
haematoma, subdural 155
haematuria 107
haemoglobin 148
haemorrhage 94
haemorrhoids 126
hair 119
hallucinations 82
Hayflick limit 39
health, failing with age 72
hearing aids 112
hearing, decline with age 44
heart, age changes 48
heart attack 135
heart block 138
heartburn 121
heart and circulation, ageing 78
heart disease 134-9
heart failure 136
heating 22
Heimlich's manoeuvre 144
herpes zoster 118
hiatus hernia 121, 122
high blood pressure 94
home help service 33
homoestasis 42, 189
hormone replacement therapy 53
    adverse effects 54
hospital car service 31
hospital services 29
housebound 169
housing associations 21
hypertension 94, 131, 139, 188

hyperthyroidism 155
hypnotic drugs 71
hypothermia 23, 102, 157
hypothyroidism 156

ileostomy 129
illness, manifestations of 74
immune system, failure 41
impotence 50
incapacity, some legal implications of 183
incontinence 103, 107
    aids 108, 109
    faecal 127
India, elderly in 7
indigestion 122
influenza, vaccine 69
insomnia 70
institutional neurosis 89
insulin 151, 152
intermittent admissions 32
intermittent claudication 99, 140
intertrigo 118
iron, deficiency 148
ischaemic heart disease 134-9

jaundice 125
joint replacement 92
joints 91

kidney, failure 106, 154
kidney function, changes with ageing 49

laxatives 126
lean body mass, shrinkage of 47
leg ulcers 119
legal aspects of incapacity 183
lenses 115
levopdopa 96
libido, loss of 52, 54
life expectancy 10, 185
life span 185
Lipofuscin 40
local authority 32
long-stay care 31
lung, changes with ageing 48

malignant disease 75, 99, 150
marathon 65

203

Index

Index

CON1 et al   Ageing: the facts

SOCIAL SCIENCE LIBRARY

Manor Road Building
Manor Road
Oxford OX1 3UQ
Tel: (2)71093 (enquiries and renewals)
http://www.ssl.ox.ac.uk

WITHDRAWN

This is a NORMAL LOAN item.

We will email you a reminder before this item is due.

Please see http://www.ssl.ox.ac.uk/lending.html
for details on:

- loan policies; these are also displayed on the
  notice boards and in our library guide.

- how to check when your books are due back.

- how to renew your books, including information
  on the maximum number of renewals.
  Items may be renewed if not reserved by
  another reader. Items must be renewed before
  the library closes on the due date.

- level of fines; fines are charged on overdue books.

Please note that this item may be recalled during Term.

300099489%